MILTON DANK

ALBERT EINSTEIN

FRANKLIN WATTS
NEW YORK | LONDON | TORONTO | SYDNEY | 1983
AN IMPACT BIOGRAPHY

A GROLIER COMPANY

Diagrams courtesy of Vantage Art, Inc.
Cover photograph courtesy of United Press International.
Photographs courtesy of:
The Bettmann Archive: pp. 5, 88, 97;
Einstein Archives: pp. 24, 31, 44, 68;
American Institute of Physics: pp. 58, 79; Brown Brothers: p. 67.

Library of Congress Cataloging in Publication Data

Dank, Milton, 1920-
Albert Einstein.

(An Impact biography)
Bibliography: p.
Includes index.
Summary: Describes Einstein's life and his work whose
impact caused a revolution in physics. Summarizes
Newton's theories and Einstein's theory of relativity.
1. Einstein, Albert, 1879-1955—Juvenile literature.
2. Physicists—Biography—Juvenile literature.
[1. Einstein, Albert, 1879-1955. 2. Physicists] I. Title.
QC16.E5D36 1983   530'.092'4   [B] [92] 82-23853
ISBN 0-531-04587-0

CONTENTS

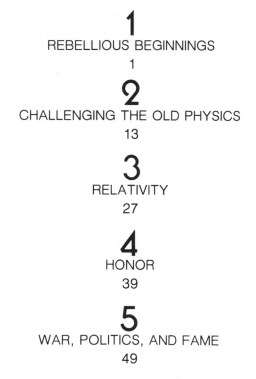

ALBERT
EINSTEIN

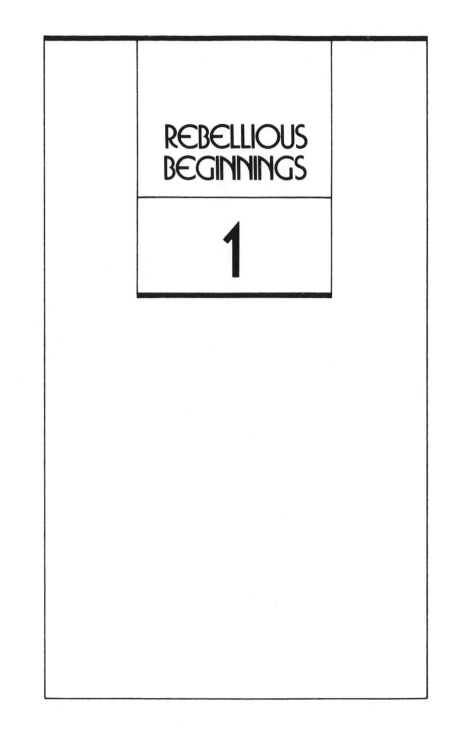

REBELLIOUS BEGINNINGS

1

Albert Einstein was born in Ulm, Germany, on March 14, 1879. No comet flashed in the skies to announce his birth. There was no sign that the equal of such scientific giants as Galileo and Newton had arrived. Not even his adoring parents could have guessed that their first child and only son would one day be called a genius. No one could have predicted that the hundredth anniversary of this birth would be celebrated around the world. Yet Albert Einstein would change forever our ideas of the world we live in. He would reveal a truer picture of the universe and the laws of nature.

His famly was in no way outstanding. The Einsteins were Jewish and had lived in southern Germany for over three hundred years. They had been tradesmen and small-business owners, prosperous but not well-known. There was not a single teacher, writer, or artist among Albert's ancestors. That such an ordinary middle-class family should produce a scientific genius is remarkable. Still, there was a Jewish tradition of great respect for scholarship and learning.

Albert's father, Hermann, was a friendly, jovial man with an easy attitude toward life. No matter how bad his business affairs were, he always felt that "something will turn up." Incurably optimistic, he would go from one business failure to another without changing his happy-go-lucky philosophy.

In 1876, Hermann Einstein married Pauline Koch, a sweet-tempered, cultured young woman. They were a devoted, happy couple with modern ideas. Like many German Jews of that time, they lived apart from the religious community. They did not join the synagogue or observe the dietary laws. They considered themselves "freethinkers," but never denied their Jewish heritage.

When Albert was born, his father was the part owner of a small company in Ulm, but Hermann's easygoing attitude did not make for success in business. In 1880, the family moved to Munich where he opened another small firm with his brother. Repeated family moves were to become an old story while Albert Einstein was growing up.

At first, the move to Munich seemed a good one. A year later, a daughter, Maria ("Maja") was born to the Einsteins and their happiness seemed complete. The business was thriving, and they had two lovely children. But soon they began to worry about their son's progress. He seemed to be so much slower in learning to talk than other children.

What we know of Einstein as a child comes from family and friends many years later when he was famous. The truth was often mixed with legend, and the two are hard to separate. Einstein himself had a tremendous memory about scientific things, but almost none about his early years. He was not even interested in recalling his childhood. He felt that a scientist's life is his work. What kind of child he was, whether he was happy or not, this was not important.

Albert Einstein
at the age of
five, with his
sister, Maja

One thing is certain: there were no signs of future genius in young Albert Einstein. He was a slow developer, late in learning to speak. He was remote and hesitant, and would take a long time thinking about a question before answering. Even when he was nine, his speech was not fluent. His troubled parents feared for a time that he was retarded.

Years later, Einstein pointed out that because of his slow development, he had not thought about many things as early as most children do. Take space and time for example: children accept these without really thinking about them. Adults tell them what to make of such ideas. Thus slow, but intelligent, learners are older and more thoughtful when they first start wondering about the nature of space and time. Albert came late to thinking about such things. This, he suggested, was why he was able to question them rather than accepting them blindly.

The world young Albert was born into was a very safe and comfortable place, and his home was a happy one. His loving parents doted on their son and his infant sister. There were grandparents, aunts, and uncles, all devoted and generous. Albert grew up in this protective circle of relatives, but thinking his own thoughts. He disliked sports and games but loved mechanical toys, especially finding out how they worked. This is the one interest that he shared with great physicists like Galileo and Newton, the two men with whom his name will be forever linked. Albert also liked jigsaw puzzles and showed an unusual manual dexterity, building tall towers of playing cards often fourteen stories tall.

When he was four or five and sick in bed, Albert received a present from his father. It was intended as an amusing toy, a diversion, but it had a profound effect. It was a magnetic compass, and his father showed him that the needle would always point in the same direction no matter how the case was turned. Another child might have become bored after playing with the compass for a while and put it aside. For Albert, however, it was a fascinating mystery. Space was not empty! There was something in the void that was gripping the iron needle and holding it fixed. Albert had no idea what a magnetic field was, but he was enchanted by the invisible force that filled what seemed to be empty space. Where did it come from? The wonder and awe of it all never left the boy or the man.

His first school was a Catholic elementary school close to his home. His "freethinking" parents had no qualms about sending their son to a convenient, cheaper school, rather than to a more distant, more expensive Jewish school. The education was as good, and they had no fear of the religious training. As the only Jewish student, young Albert was most impressed by the Bible stories. Later, this interest disappeared as he became interested in science.

That Albert Einstein was a rebellious, stubborn student in both elementary and high school is clear from his autobiography. He hated the strict discipline, the learning by memorization, and the unwillingness to consider new ideas. It was too "Prussian" for the dreamy, thoughtful boy who wanted to be left alone. He wanted to do his own thinking on the things that interested him. Later, he called his elementary school teachers "sergeants" and his high school teachers "lieutenants." He had a contempt for this type of rigid education that stayed with him all his life. His teachers must have felt this hatred, and that could not have made school a happy time for him.

Being forced to learn without questioning made him suspicious of all authority. He would criticize and doubt what his fellow students took on faith. This was probably the best preparation for his later work. It gave him the inquiring mind that would not accept something because some great name in the past had said it was so. His motto was: "How do we know that is true? Where is the proof?" That questioning attitude is the sign of a true scientific mind.

As a child, Albert was of average height, with black, curly hair and large brown eyes. There was a dreamy look in those eyes and a stubborn expression about his lips. Everyone thought him an attractive child.

Perhaps one day on a Munich street, the schoolboy hurrying to class may have passed a tall, thin, twenty-seven-year-old university teacher in a neat black suit. They would have passed each other without a glance. They would not meet again for another twenty years, but then they would both be famous. The teacher's name was Max Planck.

Albert attended elementary school until he was ten years old. His lack of attention and hesitant speech made him unpopular with his teachers. The spirit of rebellion in the boy was born here. He managed to hide his dislike of the school from his parents, but his teachers' unfavorable opinion of their "backward" pupil could not be hidden. One day, Hermann Einstein went to the school to ask the headmaster what future career his son should follow. He was told that it did not matter, for Albert would never amount to anything.

What the child did not learn in school was more than made up by what he was taught at home. His Uncle Jakob was the first to introduce him to the wonders of algebra. They made a merry game of it. His music-loving mother insisted that Albert start violin lessons at an early age. Like most children, the boy resented the laborious early training, but later, he grew to love music. As he learned more and more mathematics, he began to see mathematical relationships in the harmony. This led to a lifelong devotion to the violin, especially the music of Mozart. This musical interest is one that many scientists seem to share.

At the age of ten, Albert entered the fifth year at the Luitpold School. Here he was very unhappy. The "lieutenants" of the secondary school were no better than the "sergeants" of the elementary school. The strict obedience demanded and the minds closed to any doubt or questions repelled the boy. He became more of a "loner," an outsider. His distrust of all authority grew. Again, it was at home that his real mental growth took place.

He was beginning to sense the world around him and to wonder about it. His thoughts grew deeper and more original as his self-study increased his knowledge of science.

There was a custom at that time for a family to invite a poor Jewish student to share a meal once a week. The warm-hearted Einsteins had as their guest a medical student named Max Talmey. He was to have a strong influence on young

Albert. "A pretty, dark-haired boy with an inclination toward physics," was the way Talmey described the thirteen-year-old Einstein.

They had long talks about science and Talmey gave his young friend several popular books on science and philosophy. These Albert quickly read and understood. They made a strong impression on an eager mind and marked the real beginning of Einstein's lifelong dedication to physics. To him, it was better than any adventure story. For the first time, he was getting answers to some of the questions he had asked himself about the real world.

Understanding physics required knowing more mathematics than the boy had at that time, so Talmey gave him a beginner's geometry book. "After a short time, a few months," the medical student later wrote, "he had worked through the whole book. . . . He thereupon devoted himself to higher mathematics, studying all by himself. . . . Soon the flight of his mathematical genius was so high that I could not follow."

The teenager still refused to believe anything he read until he had proved it for himself. He questioned everything. "How do we know this is true?" and even "What is truth?" In search for the answers, he read the German philosophers who also wanted to know what truth was. What was difficult for most adults was soon clear to the eager young Albert.

He made rapid progress in his self-study so that he was well beyond the simple science and mathematics taught in class. He was never a popular student. His teachers resented his questions, and his classmates thought he was arrogant. Albert had a knowledge of his own self-worth that gave him a confident attitude. Although he spent six years at the Luitpold School, he taught himself what was important to him—physics and mathematics. More and more, his mind was turning to the problems that scientists of that day were struggling with.

At last he was thinking about things that had escaped him as a child. He was trying to understand space and time. Luckily, he could begin fresh without the old ideas that grown-ups impose on children. He knew enough science to understand why these two ideas were so puzzling.

But Albert had something else: he could hold an idea in his mind for months. He could examine the problem from different angles and make daring guesses as to the answer. This gift is what separates a genius from men of talent. It is the insight of a Galileo, a Newton, and an Einstein. These men would doggedly stay with a problem until they saw what the answer must be; then they went back and "prettied it up" with mathematics. At sixteen, Albert Einstein already had this gift—as he would prove less than ten years later.

Unhappy in school, young Albert was dealt another blow in 1894: separation from his protective family. His father's business failed. Taking their daughter, Maja, his parents moved to Italy, where his mother's wealthy relatives were willing to help the ever-optimistic Hermann Einstein start again, but under their watchful eye. Worried about their son's future career, his parents left him behind to finish high school and to get the diploma that would allow him to enter the university. They hoped he would be an electrical engineer, a well-paying profession. This seems to have been more his father's choice than Albert's, but he was too loving a son to quarrel with his father.

Placed in a boardinghouse run by a distant relative, the sixteen-year-old boy was desperately unhappy. After six months, he made up his mind to flee from the Luitpold School and Munich, and follow his family to Italy. That meant leaving before graduating and receiving his diploma. Rather than burning his bridges behind him, Albert decided to take a medical leave of absence. Somehow he managed to persuade a doctor that separation from his family had brought him to the edge of a "nervous breakdown." The sympathetic doctor gave him a medical certificate saying that a period of rest in Italy was necessary to his health.

His little plan turned out to be unnecessary. Before he could present his medical certificate, Albert was told that he was to be expelled from school. The reason given was that he was unruly in class and that his insolent, undisciplined attitude toward his teachers had affected his fellow students. Although he desperately wanted to leave, it must have been a humiliating blow to the sensitive boy. His expulsion helps to explain his later dislike of the school, his teachers, and Germany itself.

Young Einstein packed and followed his family over the Alps to Milan. His father's business soon suffered another business failure and the family moved to Pavia. Despite the money problems, it was a happy time for Albert. He loved Italy, its warm, friendly people, and its freedom. It was very different from the stifling life he had known in Munich. He did not attend school during these months. Rather he spent his time hiking through the hills wherever the spirit took him. But he was always thinking about scientific problems.

Even at this footloose time, he continued his self-study, deepening his knowledge. He was a boy who needed no teachers, for he could teach himself.

But carefree, happy days end sooner or later. His father worried about Albert's failure to prepare himself for a well-paid career. It was urgent that Albert start studying for a practical profession. He was too great a strain on the family purse.

By leaving Luitpold before getting his diploma, Albert had shut many doors to a future career. He could not hope to get into any German university. His Italian was not good enough for an Italian college, so where could he go? It had to be a school outside of Germany where German was the accepted language. It had to be a school that taught electrical engineering, for his father insisted on that training. Albert was not unhappy about a school outside of Germany. He hated the thought of compulsory military training, which was required by the German state.

Just over the Alps in Zurich, Switzerland, was a fine technical school, the Federal Institute of Technology (FIT). Entrance to the school did not require a high school diploma, but simply passing an examination. The age for entering students was eighteen and Albert was only sixteen, but he decided to try. He knew that the examination would be difficult, but he hoped that his advanced study in science would get him through. Perhaps his physics and mathematics would cover his poor understanding of every other subject on the test.

The gamble failed. Young Einstein did not pass in zoology, botany, and modern languages. His application for admission was rejected.

With his expulsion from high school and his inability to pass the examination for technical school, the future did not look bright for Albert Einstein.

CHALLENGING THE OLD PHYSICS

2

Failing the entrance examination for the FIT was a setback for Albert Einstein and a great disappointment to his family. What would become of him now? Was there to be nothing more in life for such a clever young man than a job as a clerk in a shop or in the post office?

But others had seen the test results too. Young Einstein's performance in physics and mathematics had been so outstanding that the head of the FIT urged him to spend a year studying for a degree at a nearby secondary school. This diploma would allow him to enter the FIT without taking the examination. The classes at the school in Aarau were relaxed, easygoing, and democratic, very different from what he had known in Germany. It was not difficult for him to master the work needed to earn his degree, and it left him time for his own self-study.

So content was the boy with Switzerland and so unhappy were his thoughts of Munich that he asked his father to allow him to renounce his German citizenship. This hatred of anything "Prussian" was to stay with Albert Einstein all his life. The paperwork took over a year, but when it was completed,

he was legally "a stateless person born of German parents."
He was to remain without a country until he was twenty-one,
when he became a Swiss citizen. Many years later, he would
return to his allegiance to Germany for a short time, but that is
another story.

In the summer of 1896, he had his degree from Aarau
and was admitted to the FIT. The age requirement was
waived. In the fall, he started the four-year course for teachers of physics. Finally, he knew his true lifework. Now his
father could be told that Albert would never be an electrical
engineer.

It would be nice to report that young Einstein changed his
easygoing, rebellious ways when he entered the new school.
The only thing that changed was his attendance in class—it
became worse. He quickly found that they were teaching the
old "classical" physics of Newton, which he already knew
was badly out-of-date. His teachers, however, were unaware
of the disturbing questions that had arisen about Newton's
work and refused to even think that the classical theories
might need changes. Einstein cut class to concentrate on his
own studies. Soon, he was in danger of failing the examinations. A generous friend lent him the lecture notes and, by
cramming, Einstein managed to pass.

Still, his life was not all work. On the tiny allowance he
received, Einstein could enjoy walking parties in the hills and
cheap meals with good talk in the restaurants. There were
musical evenings, with Einstein playing the violin and Mileva
Maric, a fellow student from Serbia, playing the piano. Mileva
was only one of the young women who found the curly-haired,
plump-cheeked Albert fascinating. However, she was the one
he would later marry.

Other than these few hours of relaxation, Einstein had no
time for anything but his work. His self-study, his thinking
about problems in physics, came first. Everything else—even
eating and sleeping—came second. When he went for a sail-
boat ride on one of the nearby lakes, he always carried a
notebook in his pocket. If the wind died, out came the note-

book and he would work feverishly until the wind came up again. He knew that there was a revolution coming, a scientific revolution, and he was getting ready for the struggle.

It is difficult to trace the course of his thinking during these critical years, for he wrote little about them in his autobiography. But we do know what was going on in physics between 1896 and 1900. In his classes, Einstein listened to lectures—when he attended—on the "old" physics. Outside of class, Einstein studied the newest discoveries. He learned of the questions that were being asked about the very foundations of classical physics. It was clear that something was very wrong with the physical laws that his teachers held sacred. It was becoming clear to Einstein that the questions could not be answered without big changes in the great structure that Newton had built.

Disputing a giant like Newton did not bother the seventeen-year-old rebel. He kept asking himself the same question over and over: "How do we know this is true?" Now he had the problem in his mind, and he would not let go until he had the answer. And it had to be the right answer and not just the one his teachers tried to hand him because it was Newton's answer.

To understand Einstein's contribution to scientific thought we have to know something about the "old" physics.

The ancient Greek philosophers began science by thinking deeply about nature. They did few experiments because only slaves worked with their hands. Nevertheless, the Greeks learned a great deal about science and mathematics. Euclid put all of plane geometry in one book. Democritus had the idea that all matter was made of something like atoms. When the philosophers were wrong—as they were about the laws of motion—it was from a failure to define basic concepts and to confirm their theories by experiment.

Modern science began with Galileo Galilei, who was born in Florence, Italy, in 1564. To him we owe the idea that the truth of any physical law can be determined only by experiment. He corrected many of the errors about the motion of bodies that had persisted for two thousand years.

The Greeks had said that heavier objects fell faster than light ones. Look at the fall of a feather and a lead ball, they said. It is only common sense. Galileo guessed that all objects fall at the same speed and only air resistance slows down the feather more. Unfortunately, he could not produce a good vacuum to prove this by experiment. The story of his dropping two unequal weights from the Leaning Tower of Pisa is probably a legend. Even if he had done it, the experiment would have proved nothing. But Galileo had the insight of genius. He knew what the right answer had to be.

The Greeks claimed that to keep a body moving, a constant push or pull (which we call a "force") is needed. Again it seemed obvious to them. If you stop pushing or pulling a cart on flat ground, it will stop moving.

"Not so," said Galileo. "Again you forgot about friction, this time of the ground. Without that friction, the cart will gain speed as long as you push or pull it. Once you stop, the cart will keep going at a steady speed. If it is at rest, it will stay so until you push or pull it."

You might say that Einstein's theory of relativity started with this simple but important law. If there is no push-pull, an object at rest stays at rest; an object in motion continues to move in a straight line with an unchanging speed. This property of a body that resists changes in its state of motion unless acted on by a force is called its "inertia."

Suppose you are traveling in a windowless railroad car that is moving on a perfectly smooth flat track at a constant speed in a straight line (uniform motion). Since you cannot look out and see the telephone poles whizzing by, can you tell if you are moving or at rest with respect to the ground? Galileo's law of inertia says no. Only if some force acts (the train accelerates and you lurch or the car hits a bump that throws you upward) will you know that you are moving relative to the ground.

All motion is relative to something (which we call a "reference frame"). It makes no sense to talk of a body moving unless we specify the reference frame it is moving relative to. If you throw this book across the room, it is moving relative to the walls and floor. Its position at any instant can be given by its shortest distance from any two touching walls and the floor. Since we need only three numbers to locate the book at a given instant of time, we say that space is three-dimensional.

Any frame of reference in which Galileo's law of inertia is valid is called an "inertial frame of reference." Suppose you make a window in your closed railroad car and see a man standing beside the track. You both are in your own inertial frames of reference that are in relative uniform motion. Which of you is at rest and which is in motion? You say it is the man on the "fixed" ground who is at rest and you are speeding by him. But can you prove that? Suppose you are at rest and he is speeding past you. Again we must give the reference frame for this motion. Clearly you are at rest in your frame (the railroad car), and the man is at rest in his frame (the ground). What we need is an "absolute" fixed frame of reference to which we can refer both motions. Maybe one of you is at rest with respect to this absolute reference system.

This question of the existence of an absolute frame of reference plays a vital role in our story.

Galileo died in 1642, the year the English physicist Isaac Newton was born. Starting with Galileo's ideas, Newton brilliantly made a real science of moving bodies. He showed that the fall of a pebble and the motion of the planets around the sun both came from the pull of gravity. He explained how the push-pull of a force changed the speed of a body. He did marvelous work on the nature of light, and the higher mathematics called calculus was his invention. Newton was a scientific genius of the first order. He was also a very religious man who dedicated his work to the glory of God. It was God, he thought, who was the Originator of space and time. It was God who had wound up this wonderful clockwork that was the universe.

For the discovery of his universal laws, Newton was praised and honored as no scientist had ever been. A poet of the time wrote:

Nature and Nature's laws lay hid in night:
God said: Let Newton be! and all was light.

No one wanted to quibble with the man who had proved that the planets and the legendary falling apple obeyed the same simple law of gravity. But even at that time, there were some who were worried about Newton's ideas. Take his idea that gravity acts immediately between two bodies. That means that if you move this book 1 inch (2.54 cm), every other body in the universe is instantly aware of this movement through a change in the pull of gravity!

What sort of pull-force could act that quickly? It would have to be faster than the speed of light.

And some scientists were unhappy with Newton's idea of space as something that existed in God's mind, and of time as a river that flowed from the beginning to the end. It was all very puzzling, but nothing succeeded like Newton's success. The people who complained were thought to be jealous of his fame (Appendix A).

Newton thought that light was a stream of particles called "luminiferous corpuscles." Later, this idea was discarded by scientists when experiments showed that light was a wave. By the nineteenth century, light was proved to be an "electromagnetic" wave—a combination of electric and magnetic fields moving at 186,000 miles (299,000 km) per second. This raised a serious problem.

Unlike sound and water waves, light goes through a vacuum. There had to be some material for the light wave to move in, so they invented one and called it the "ether." It was an invisible jelly that quivered as light waves passed through it. It filled all space. The planets, the sun, and the galaxies could whirl through it without disturbing it. It was inside glass, air, water, and a vacuum. It had to be present, since light could go through all these materials. A very strange thing, the "ether."

By Einstein's day, the ether was in trouble. Very careful experiments had been done to detect it (Appendix B), and they had all failed. All explanations for the failure were proven wrong. People tried desperately to keep the ether, for without it they would not know how to explain light. There had to be something to carry the light waves.

Let's try to simplify these ideas about space, time, and light. Here is a "thought experiment" just like the ones Einstein puzzled over.

We have two men whom we will call "observers." Observer A is standing on a railroad platform, and observer B is passing by on a train. The train is moving in a straight line at a constant speed. Therefore, A and B are in uniform motion relative to one another. Both men are holding a yardstick in one hand and a clock in the other. The two clocks were synchronized earlier. As the train passes the platform, each man measures the yardstick and records the time of the other. What do they find?

According to Newton, they both find the other's yardstick to be exactly 1 yard (0.91 m) and the other's clock to be still synchronized with his own. In other words, the relative uniform motion had no effect on the measurement of space and time.

Now, B fires a gun toward the front of the train. Both men measure the bullets speed—and get different answers! This means that the relative uniform motion has an effect on what the two men measure (Appendix A). This is Newton's "addition of velocities."

B shines a flashlight toward the front of the train. Both men measure the speed of the light beam. They both find it is exactly 186,000 miles (299,000 km) per second! Newton's law for the addition of velocities does not apply to light! Yet it works so well for everything else, why not for light? Why doesn't the speed of light depend on the speed of the flashlight?

These were the problems that puzzled many scientists at the end of the nineteenth century. None of this was even discussed at the FIT, so Einstein had to figure it out for himself. Why could the ether not be detected? Why did light not follow Newton's law for adding velocities? What were space and time really?

Four years at the Swiss Federal Institute of Technology did not endear Albert Einstein to his teachers. They found him stubborn, unwilling to accept anything without questioning it, and reluctant to study any subject that did not interest him. That meant almost everything outside of physics and the mathematics he needed.

He was a poor experimenter, inept in the laboratory. Once he tore up the instructions and tried to do the experiment his own way. He seriously injured his hand, but persisted in seeking new, quicker ways to do the work. In his understanding of the latest advances in physics, he was far ahead of his teachers, and when he proposed to build an apparatus to detect the "ether," they pooh-poohed the idea.

We have a clear picture of what he looked like from his fellow students, not all of whom liked him. He was 5 feet 9 inches (1.75 m) tall with black, curly hair and a narrow mustache. His mouth was wide, his nose straight, and his shoulders broad. He walked with a slight stoop. Most people mentioned his eyes—brown with a friendly, dreamy look—and his soft, vibrant speaking voice. He always seemed to be thinking deep thoughts even in casual conversations with his friends. Time for his self-study was important to him, and his sharp tongue discouraged intruders. Yet his laughter and his sense of humor were remembered by many who knew him in those days.

In August 1900, Einstein graduated from the FIT with an average grade of 82 percent, not a particularly distinguished academic record. His teachers thought that he was a clever young man, but unteachable, for he would not listen to his elders. Not one of them thought Einstein had any chance of success as a teacher or as a physicist. Not one of them wrote a recommendation for him.

For the twenty-one-year-old graduate, the end of his school days brought severe money problems. His allowance from his family now ended, and he was expected to find a job and make his own way. The final examinations had given the young man such a distaste for scientific work that it was a whole year before he could consider physics again. All his friends found jobs of one sort or another in their chosen fields, but not Albert Einstein. No one wanted to employ a man on whom his teachers had turned thumbs down.

Lacking money, he went back to his family in Milan and wrote letters to well-known professors, asking for a job as an assistant. All he had to offer as credentials were several papers that had been published in the German *Annals of Physics*. He knew that they were not outstanding works (later he referred to them as worthless), but he had nothing else to show. How do you prove that you are a genius in a job application?

He returned to Switzerland and supported himself by part-time teaching and tutoring. His application for Swiss citizenship was granted in February 1901, after an examining board found that he was too naive and absentminded to be a revolutionary. All Swiss citizens had to serve in the army, but Einstein was rejected for flat feet and varicose veins. One wonders what his officers would have made of him if he had been accepted.

Soon things became very desperate for the struggling young physicist. The little part-time work he had been able to find dried up. With no money and no help from his family or relatives, he had to find a job, and soon.

At this low point in his life, an old friend gave him a helping hand and earned his eternal gratitude. It was the same fellow student who had lent him the lecture notes that had allowed Einstein to cram for his examinations. His name was Marcel Grossmann, and his father knew the head of the Swiss Patent Office in Bern. There would soon be an opening for an examiner, second class. The pay was small but Einstein needed regular work, so he applied for the position as soon as it was advertised. Although he did not have the engineering background needed, he impressed the interviewers with his knowledge of higher mathematics and the new physics. Einstein had to wait seven months before the job was offered to him and then it was as an examiner, *third* class, at an even

smaller salary. He accepted without hesitation. It was the only position offered to him, and besides he wanted to get married.

The work in the Federal Patent Office turned out to be to Einstein's liking. It was his job to inspect the applications for patents, which included blueprints of the claimed invention plus a working model. Even knowing little engineering, he could quickly grasp the physical principles involved and determine whether the things could work or not. His superiors were impressed with the speed with which he went through a pile of applications. What they did not know was that the young examiner, third class, was using some of his free time to do his own calculations. These he would scribble on bits of paper that could be shoved in a drawer when a superior passed by. Einstein was happy. He still had the small boy's love of mechanical toys—which is what the models were to him. Also, he felt that one should not be paid for doing physics. It was better to have another job and do what he wanted to do out of love for science.

In January 1903, he married Mileva Maric, his Serbian fellow student at the FIT. It was not a happy marriage despite the birth of two sons. Four years older than her husband, the gloomy, suspicious young wife was unable to provide the quiet home life that Einstein needed for his work. Perhaps as a physicist, Mileva felt that she should share in her husband's triumphs (like the Curies), but she could not grasp his theories. Einstein refused to take the time to explain them. It was an unfortunate marriage and in time the Einsteins realized that it was a mistake. Like most unhappy couples, they struggled along together, trying to hide their failure from others.

Einstein's marriage to
Mileva Maric in 1903 proved
to be an unhappy one. Here
he poses with his wife and
their first son, Hans Albert.

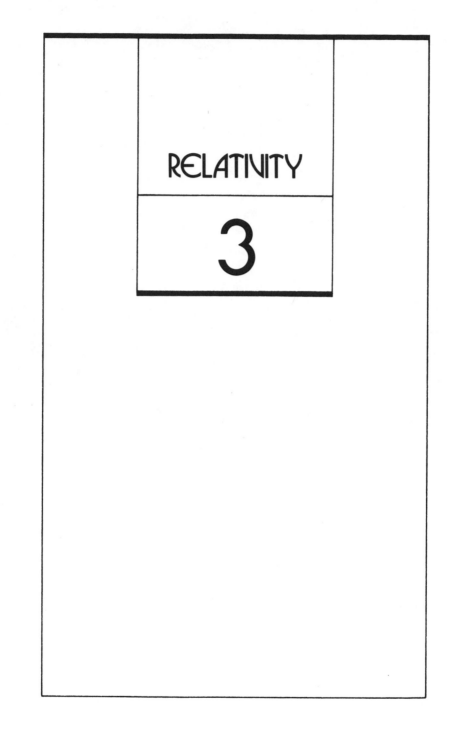

RELATIVITY

3

There are two "miraculous years" in the history of science. One was 1666, when the twenty-four-year-old Isaac Newton fled the plague in Cambridge to his mother's country home. Here he did his most brilliant work on moving bodies and gravity. The second "miraculous year" was 1905, when Albert Einstein published simultaneously four papers that changed our view of the world forever.

Despite his full-time job at the patent office, financial worries, and personal problems in his marriage, Einstein finished these four papers in one year. If he had done only the one on special relativity, he would have been famous. To have done four was miraculous.

Let us look briefly at the first three papers. Although important, they are not as earthshaking as the paper on relativity.

If you look at a mixture of fine dust and water under a microscope, each particle of dust has a wiggling movement that never stops. Einstein proved that the particle was being bombarded on all sides by molecules of water. This was like moving a basketball by firing BBs at it from all directions. This paper helped convince many scientists of the existence of atoms and molecules, a controversial subject at that time.

The second paper dealt with the electrons that come out of a metal plate when light shines on it (the "photoelectric effect"). A German physicist, Philipp Lenard, had found that stronger light made more electrons come out, but at the same speed. He had to use bluer light to get the electrons to come out faster. No one could explain this.

Einstein had heard of the work of Max Planck. Five years earlier, Planck had shown that light was discontinuous, granular. He called the grains "quanta" (from the Greek for "how much"). This sounded like Newton's idea that light consisted of "luminiferous corpuscles." Einstein used Planck's quanta of light (which he renamed "photons") to explain Lenard's results. It worked beautifully. Unfortunately, it left the unsettled problem of how light could be both a wave and a particle. This would return in later years to bother Einstein.

The third paper dealt with a way of finding the size of molecules and is the least important of the four. Yet this was Einstein's thesis for the Ph.D. degree he received from the University of Zurich.

The fourth paper was actually the third one to be published that year. It carries the heavy title of "On the Electrodynamics of Moving Bodies." Today we know it as the "special theory of relativity."

We have mentioned the sort of problems that were puzzling physicists at that time. Einstein had been thinking about

Albert Einstein,
at his desk in the
Bern Patent Office,
around the time he
published his paper
on the special
theory of relativity.

the "ether," about why light did not obey Newton's law for the addition of velocities, and especially about space and time. His intuition told him that the answer to the first two problems was in the third. There was something wrong with Newton's ideas about space and time. Remember that Newton could not define these two ideas (Appendix A). He left that to God. Because of Newton's success, most scientists had swept the problem under the rug. "God and Newton understand what space and time are, and that's good enough for us," was the attitude of all but a few scientists for over a hundred years. It was not good enough for Albert Einstein. In 1905, he would pull back the rug and sweep away the mistakes.

In 1905, Einstein was twenty-five years old, but he had been thinking about these problems since he was sixteen. There is a story about how the teenaged Einstein tackled such weighty problems that shows how his mind worked.

According to this story, young Einstein was riding in a trolley car in Munich. He looked back at the clock in the steeple of City Hall as the trolley car moved away from it and asked himself, "What is time? The time I see on that clock is known to me because light has hit the clock face and then traveled to my eye. But the speed of light is not infinite. In fact, I know the exact value: 186,000 miles (299,000 km) per second. While the light is traveling to my eye, the trolley is moving away. When the light hits my eye, I see the clock face not as it is at that exact instant, but as it was a tiny fraction of a second earlier. This makes no important difference because I am close to the clock, the trolley is moving very slowly, and the speed of light is so great.

"But suppose the trolley were to move faster and faster? Then the error would increase, a minute would seem to get longer. In fact, the clock would seem to be slowing down! And if I were to move at the speed of light, the light from the clock face would never reach me and I would think that the clock had stopped! Yet according to Newton, this can never happen. He says that time is a constantly flowing river that is independent of the speed of the observer. . . ."

This story may not be true, but it certainly shows the sort

of thinking that Einstein excelled at. It is called a "thought experiment" and requires no equipment or apparatus at all. Obviously Einstein could not move at the speed of light to prove that the clock would appear to have stopped, but there was nothing to stop him from going step-by-step and guessing that the clock would seem to be going slower and slower. If the thought experiment was correct, Newton was wrong about the nature of time.

There was another puzzle Einstein tackled. Experiments hinted that light did not obey Newton's law for the addition of velocities (see Appendix B). Either something was wrong with the theory of light or else Newton's law was wrong. Which one?

Skipping lectures and cramming for examinations, Einstein struggled with these problems. The electromagnetic theory of light was not taught at the FIT, but he had started to learn it by himself at the Aarau school. There he had a "thought experiment" about the mysterious light wave.

"What would happen," he wondered, "if I were to travel at the speed of light and look at a light wave?" It would seem to have stopped. But that is impossible. The speed of light never changes. It can't stand still."

These ideas were the beginnings of his own theory of relativity. Even as a student, Einstein had the problem fixed in his mind. He would work on it for ten years before he had the answer.

Now we will outline the results of Einstein's special theory of relativity. In Appendix C, a fuller explanation of how he arrived at these results is given.

It was Einstein's genius, his intuition, that told him that the answer to all these problems involved the following question: What do we mean when we say that two things happen at the same time?

This question seems rather silly. The answer is obvious. We look at the two things and we see that they happen at the same time. Einstein thought deeper about this and came up with a different answer.

He did another of his "thought experiments." Suppose

the two events, the happenings, are far apart. How can an observer tell if they happen at the same time? Well, you might say, put the observer exactly midway between the two events. If light from each event arrives at the same time at the midpoint, we can say that the two events happened at the same time. Agreed, Einstein said, but what about another observer who is speeding by in a train? Do the two events happen at the same time for that observer?

Einstein found that the answer to the last question is no. The two observers do not see the same thing. When the observer at the midpoint says the events happen at the same time, the observer on the train says they do not. And the reason is clear: The observer on the train is moving toward one of the events and that light will get to her before the light from the event she is moving away from.

Now we see why this is called a theory of relativity. The description of "simultaneous" events depends on relative motion. It is different for observers moving relative to one another.

Having done the "thought experiment" and arrived at this startling conclusion, Einstein could now use mathematics to find the other results of his discovery. They were startling, even astonishing. He found that when one observer was in uniform motion with respect to another, they saw very different things.

Suppose two men each held a yardstick and a clock. The second man would find that the first man's ruler was less than a yard (0.91 m) long and that the first man's clock was running slow compared to his yardstick and clock (Appendix C). And the first man would say the same thing about the second man's yardstick and clock! Each one would say that lengths (in the direction of their relative motion) had shrunk and that the other's clock was running slow.

Also, the mass of a body—that is, the amount of matter that gives it its weight—appears to change with relative motion. As the relative speeds of the two men increases, each will think that objects held by the other weigh more. So, an electron speeding down a tube weighs more than you would find if you were speeding down the tube with it!

Einstein found the equations by which one man could calculate what was going on in the other man's space. These equations came from the assumption Einstein had started with—that the speed of light would always be measured at 186,000 miles (299,000 km) per second no matter how large the relative motion. Even if one observer was moving close to the speed of light relative to another observer, he would measure the speed of light in the other man's space as exactly 186,000 miles (299,000 km) per second, and vice versa. From these "transformation" equations came a new "addition of velocities" law that differed significantly from Newton's at very high speeds.

If lengths (yardsticks), time (clocks), and mass change with the observer's speed, what kind of space is this? Four dimensions are needed, the mathematician Minkowski found, instead of Newton's three dimensions. To locate the corner of this book in the room you are in, it is no longer enough to give three numbers—the distances of the edge of the book from two walls and the floor. No, that is the old physics, and it does not work because distances change with the motion of the observer. Now you must also give a fourth number, which is the speed of light multiplied by time. Which time? The time at which you are measuring the location of the edge of this book. And if you make several measurements, the time will be different but not the other three dimensions, unless you move the book.

The "ether" disappeared, thrown into the trash can with all the other discarded ideas in the old physics. The speed of light was constant, never changing—according to Einstein, that was a law of nature. So there could be no "ether wind" to slow up a light beam and thus no "ether" (see Appendix B).

Why did it take so long to discover these effects of relativity? The answer is: they are very, very small at ordinary speeds. For the mass of a body to increase one per cent, it must go one-seventh of the speed of light. That means moving at over 26,000 miles (42,000 km) per second. And at that speed, lengths will shrink 1 percent (in the direction of the motion) and clocks will be 1 percent slow. But 26,000 miles

(42,000 km) per second is almost 94,000,000 miles (151,000,000 km) per hour!

A jet plane goes about 600 miles (1,000 km) per hour; this is only 1/6 mile (0.27 km) per second. A satellite going 24,000 miles (39,000 km) per hour is only going 6 2/3 miles (10.7 km) per second. Compare this with the speed of light which is 186,000 miles (299,000 km) per second, and it is easy to see how small these relativity effects are.

That is why Newton's laws are still taught in school even after Einstein had shown them to be incomplete. In everyday life, at ordinary speeds, the difference between Newton's answer to a problem and Einstein's answer is very small. For practical purposes, the difference can be ignored. If we want to study the flight of a cannonball or a spaceship, Newton's laws work very well. The relativity corrections are tiny, most of them too small to be detected or measured.

Then why bother learning about Einstein's relativity? Because there is a whole world outside of everyday experience, a world in which bodies move at fantastic speeds close to the speed of light. This is the world of the atom and the nucleus, where we find the tiny particles of which all matter is made. In this world, we must use Einstein's relativity and not Newton's to get the right answer.

So far we have talked about bodies moving in a straight line at a constant speed. Later, Einstein thought of observers moving with changing speeds and developed a "general relativity" that applies not to the very small, but to the very large—the solar system, the stars, and the galaxies.

If he had done nothing more than devise the special theory of relativity, Albert Einstein would still have ranked among the greatest names in physics. If he had died in 1906, he would still be remembered and praised. Fortunately, he would live another fifty years.

The importance of his papers was not immediately clear to most of the scientists of his day. There was very little comment about them. First of all, the work of a Swiss patent clerk was not something that the renowned professors at the big universities thought important. No one likes a "pushy" newcomer. Second, the ideas were hard to grasp and completely contrary to the ideas of the old physics. To dispute Newton was heresy. Very slowly, people began to discuss these strange ideas, and more and more they began to ask, "Who is this man Einstein?"

Back in Bern, the patent clerk worked during the day examining applications. The rest of the time he devoted to his original studies. If he was disappointed that his papers did not bring him instant fame and job offers, he did not show it. His single-minded concentration, his refusal to allow the petty concerns of everyday life to rob him of the precious hours of thought put great strain on his marriage. What he wanted from a wife was the freedom to do his work without having to worry about the household, the children, his food, and his clothing. What his wife wanted was a partnership she could never have with an Einstein. In the world he had entered, she could not follow.

HONOR

4

After such a brilliant beginning, one might have expected Einstein to be exhausted and willing to take a rest. Instead, he worked harder than ever to probe all the consequences of his new ideas. It did not bother him that these ideas were not being received with open arms. He knew they were true and important, and that is what counted.

In the same "miraculous year," he published another paper that has affected the life of every human being and will continue to do so for all time. It came out of his special theory of relativity, again through a "thought experiment," and seemed unprovable by experiment. "What happens," he asked, "when an atom changes by sending out light rays?" He found that the light carried off energy and that the mass of the atom decreased. This led to the most famous formula in physics: $E = mc^2$. The light energy was equal to the change in the mass multiplied by the square of the speed of light. This meant that energy and mass were the same! Mass could be thought of as frozen energy!

Because of the enormous factor of the square of the speed of light, the loss of a tiny bit of mass means the release of fantastically large amount of energy. The atom bomb and the horror of nuclear war, Hiroshima and Nagasaki, all lie in this simple equation. Einstein could not see it; no man could, no matter how powerful his intuition and insight. Besides, there was no way to test the equation. In 1905—and for many years after—it would be impossible to measure such a small loss of mass in an atom. It seemed to be just a curious result of relativity theory without any real consequences.

And it was not only relativity theory that Einstein was expanding. There was also his bold idea of photons, his picture of light as a stream of particles. Even Planck, who had discovered this effect, was alarmed at how far Einstein was taking this idea. But Einstein saw deeper into Planck's work than even Planck did. The explanation and success in applying photons to the photoelectric effect gave Einstein new insight into the nature of solid materials. If light, which appears to be continuous, is really made up of individual particles, maybe this is a law of nature! The atoms that make up a solid were thought to vibrate at all frequencies, but suppose this is not so. Suppose only certain vibrations were allowed.

Using these ideas, Einstein was able to explain some peculiar behavior of solids at very low termperatures.

All this was changing the old classical physics. No wonder most of the scientific leaders looked on him with alarm. All their lives they had lived and worked within the great framework of Newtonian physics. Now this young unknown was changing all this.

Still, the success of Einstein's ideas could not be denied. Who else could explain why the ether could not be found? The jiggling of dust in water? The speed of electrons from a metal plate when light shines upon it? Solids at low temperature? Theories that agree so closely with experiments have to be taken seriously no matter who proposes them.

Slowly over the next four years, people began to talk about the new bright star of the new physics. Some came to Bern to visit him and were astonished to find that he was not at the university. When they came to the patent office and found him working at his desk in shirt sleeves, surrounded by piles of patent applications, it was hard for them to believe that this dark-haired young man was a great revolutionary.

Planck was converted to relativity, but not to photons. He was still trying to find a way to explain them according to the old physics. After all, there was still the puzzling wave form of light. How could light be both wave and particle? Unknown to both men, this question would not be answered for twenty years. The answer would satisfy neither man. To Einstein, the solution to this problem was just plain wrong, and he would end his career attacking it.

But all this was in the future, and despite his growing fame among the top men in his field, Albert Einstein still had to make a living. Separated from the great centers of learning, without even a decent technical library to use in his work, he wanted a job in a university where he would find men who would understand what he was trying to do. Not that his superiors were unaware of the budding genius in their midst. They rewarded him for his accomplishments by making him an engineer, second class! A grand promotion in their eyes for a man with only a year's experience.

In 1908, Einstein became a part-time teacher at Bern University. It was an unpaid post, depending on the students who took his course to pay a fee. Since he was a poor lecturer, too absorbed in his own thoughts, he received little money and less prestige. Still, it was the first rung on the academic ladder.

A year later, his growing fame brought him an offer from the University of Zurich. At the age of thirty, he was made associate professor of theoretical physics, a great step upward. Finally, after seven years in the patent office, he felt secure enough to resign from his post as engineer, second class. While he looked forward to the university, he had very fond memories of his days examining inventions and of sneaking in his own calculations when his superiors were not watching. He never got over the notion that one should not be paid for doing such wonderful work as theoretical physics.

Being a professor at the University of Zurich was very different from being a patent clerk. With his new prestige,

Einstein found himself being treated as an equal by the top men in his field. He was invited to meetings where relativity and photons were attacked by famous men. He found to his delight that he was able to stand up to them and refute their arguments. While he had never lacked self-confidence, this was the first time he had met these men face-to-face. That he could hold his own in such distinguished company was a great source of satisfaction after the isolation of Bern.

His fame increased when new experiments on the photoelectric effect strengthened his photon theory. Now he was recognized as the coming man, the brightest star after a meteoric rise. He corresponded with all the outstanding physicists of his day, preaching his new ideas and countering arguments against them. Universities vied to get this young man on their faculties. Offers poured in from Vienna, from the Netherlands (where the famous H.A. Lorentz wanted him as a successor at Leiden), from Utrecht, and from Prague, where the German university offered him a full professorship. Einstein spent eighteen months at Prague, but his academic wandering was not yet ended.

In October 1912, Albert Einstein returned to the Swiss Federal Institute of Technology in Zurich. It must have pleased him to return as full professor to the very school that had failed him on his first entrance examination seventeen years earlier. One wonders what his teachers—those who were still there—made of the triumphant return of the student who "would not listen to anyone."

His move from Prague may have been brought about by his wife's unhappiness there and her love for Switzerland. As a poor Serbian student, she had been happy studying at the FIT and may have thought that her foundering marriage might have a better chance to survive there. This is only a guess, for Einstein was not usually a man to worry about his wife's wishes in these matters.

Before leaving for Zurich, Einstein was invited to a Brussels conference of the most important physicists. The Belgian chemist and manufacturer Ernest Solvay had been persuaded to fund this meeting to discuss important topics, including relativity and photon theories. It was a long, tiring meeting,

At the First Solvay Congress in 1911, Einstein (standing, second from right) took his place among the leading physicists of his day.

five days of speeches and arguments, sometimes a bit hot and excited. Lorentz was the chairman and tried to keep order, but these men and Madame Curie, the only woman, felt deeply about these matters. Einstein was listened to respectfully, but his opponents did not give an inch in their objections to his new ideas. Still Einstein had his defenders too, Planck and Lorentz among them.

In any case, it was clear that Einstein had arrived and was now to be numbered among the leaders in his field. There would be no more sneers at the "Swiss patent clerk," for his accomplishments were too clear, his work too important. If not the first in theoretical physics, then certainly he was among the top three. This was a man to be reckoned with, even to be jealous of. His clear presentation of his ideas, his brilliant intuition, his grasp of what was at the heart of a problem, and his humility—all these made a deep impression.

The First Solvay Congress was a big success, and the participants planned to meet again in two years. No one doubted that at that time Albert Einstein would have new marvels to tell them.

Returning to Zurich, Einstein picked up the work on extending his ideas on relativity. The special theory of relativity was just that: a special case that could be applied only to observers moving at different constant speeds. What happens when the speeds change? What happens when one observer accelerates (or decelerates) with respect to the other? Does he see an experiment differently from the other observer? The mathematics in this new situation turned out to be much more difficult than for the special theory, but Einstein used his insight, his "thought experiments," to show where the answer must be. While he was hard at work, other men were planning to grab this rising young scientist for their schools.

Max Planck was one of them. He believed in relativity and fought for Einstein's strange ideas against the unbelievers. In spite of the fact that Planck himself had discovered that light was a stream of particles, he could not believe in the elusive photons. Rather than destroy the old physics, he was working desperately to find another answer. He recognized Einstein's genius and was willing to consider the younger man's photon theory as one of those mistakes that even the greatest of physicists can be allowed to make from time to time. After all, even Newton had been wrong about space and time.

Planck was determined to bring Einstein to Berlin. The German emperor, Kaiser Wilhelm II, had graciously allowed his name to be used for a series of scientific institutes to be set up in Berlin. Planck wanted Einstein as head of the scientific research department of the new Kaiser Wilhelm Institute of Physics. He talked to all the important people, urging them to support his efforts. He pointed out what Einstein had already done at such an early age and what wonderful things he would do in the future. He talked of the prestige that would come to Germany if these marvels were done by Einstein in Berlin. What if this deep thinker was a Swiss citizen and a Jew, was that important? After all, he had been born in Germany, and everyone would soon think of him as a German working in the land of his birth.

To make the job even more attractive, in addition to heading the research department at the Institute of Physics, Einstein would be made a member of the famous Royal Prussian Academy of Science and would have nothing to do but concentrate on his work. Berlin was at that time the center of scientific research. Students came from all over the world to study with the famous professors there. Einstein would be surrounded by men capable of understanding what he was trying to do, men with worldwide reputations. The salary was generous, the duties were light, the prestige was enormous. How could a mere professor at Zurich turn down such an offer?

Since a refusal by Einstein would be a personal insult to the kaiser, Planck went to Switzerland to make the offer in person. Einstein admired Planck, appreciated his support for relativity, and understood his opposition to photons. He was dazzled by the offer. He was only thirty-five years old, and he was being offered one of the most honored scientific positions in the world. Not only would he have freedom from the teaching chores he disliked, but he would have the best physicists in the world as colleagues. There would be men around him he could talk to as an equal, men who would grasp what he was aiming at. Also, the money would free him from the constant worry about supporting his family.

But Einstein had certain reservations. He told Planck that he would insist on keeping his Swiss citizenship and on being recognized as a Jew. This was not a matter of religion for Einstein, who observed no religion, but a recognition of the anti-Jewish sentiments in Germany. He would not go there under false colors.

What he did not mention to Planck was a family matter. His wife hated Germany. Moving to Berlin would put an even greater strain on his shaky marriage. Einstein would not let this stand in his way if he decided to accept the offer, but he disliked the thought of the quarrels it would bring.

Planck returned to Berlin with Einstein's conditions. It was not easy to get the kaiser's consent to allow such a great German institution to be headed by a Swiss Jew, but Einstein was too big a prize to miss. The kaiser agreed, and the formal offer was made. Despite his wife's objections, Einstein accepted. He knew his work was important and was willing to sacrifice his personal life to help his research. He had a vision of how the universe was built, and like a prophet he had to follow where it led.

In April 1914, the Einsteins moved to Berlin. As great as his fame was among the top men in his field, Albert Einstein was little known to the man in the street. The theory of relativity was buried in scientific journals. Almost nothing about it was printed in the newspapers or magazines. Besides, who but a trained physicist would have understood it?

Berlin held no charms for Mileva Einstein. Her husband had his work and his colleagues at the institute. Although she was a physicist, she was still denied any role in her husband's research. He made it clear that her job was to run the house, take care of their two sons, and free him from the petty annoyances of everyday life.

In the summer of 1914, she took the children to Switzerland for a vacation. Perhaps she intended to return, but events prevented it. In any case, it was soon clear that the marriage was over.

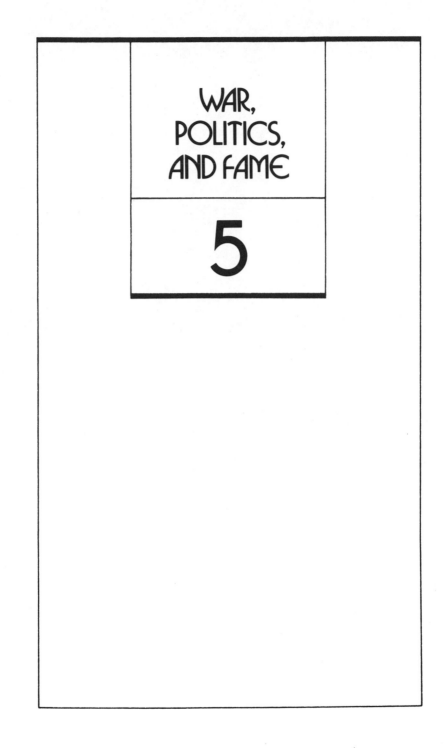

WAR,
POLITICS,
AND FAME

5

In August 1914, the First World War began. In the streets of Berlin, Paris, Vienna, Moscow, and London, patriotic crowds cheered feverishly as the troops marched off to battle. The civilized world was plunging into a four-year slaughter in the trenches with the cry of "Victory!" on its lips.

Albert Einstein was a pacifist with a profound hatred of war. He had never trusted the "Prussians," and he was deeply shocked when Germany joined the war by invading neutral Belgium. All around him, men were going mad. Hysteria was in the air, and hatred of the enemy was the order of the day. Einstein had no enemy to hate. He isolated himself in his research, refusing to be drawn into helping the war effort. He was not at all reluctant to let his hatred of all wars be known, and only his Swiss citizenship saved him from being attacked.

The war had an immediate disastrous effect on the friendships among scientists around the world. German scientists no longer felt that French and English scientists were colleagues, and vice versa. The feeling that science was above the petty quarrels of nations disappeared when the first bugle sounded the call to arms. It seemed that most scientists were as affected by "patriotism" and the glamor of war as any man in the street. On both sides of the battle line, men who had dedicated their lives to the pursuit of scientific truth rushed to offer their knowledge to their government. All their learning would be given to finding better ways to kill their fellowman. To Einstein, it was a terrible sin. It disgusted him, for he had thought that scientists were a higher form of human being. In the two World Wars, they would prove him wrong.

The war also isolated and separated the scientists. Cut off from writing to colleagues in England and France, Einstein could keep up with work in those countries—the little pure physics that was done during the war—only through his friends in neutral Holland and Switzerland. It was a blow, for he was still trying to convince many of them of the truth of his work. He was heartsick to learn that so many men that he admired were now working on guns, airplanes, and even poison gas. To him, this use of science was worse than a sin.

To justify Germany's role in the war, a pleading document titled "Manifesto to the Civilized World" was published by a group of scientists. It made the unbelievable claim that imperial Germany was fighting to defend civilization against barbarians and called on the world community of scientists to support the struggle. It was signed by ninety-three German scientists, all with worldwide reputations. Planck was one of them, although he may have done so reluctantly. As a Swiss, Einstein was not asked to sign. Besides, his sentiments were well-known, and the signers did not want to risk his public refusal.

But Einstein was not willing to let the "Manifesto to the Civilized World" go unanswered. Not signing it was not enough for such an insult to science. With three other German scientists, he wrote and signed a "Manifesto to Europeans." This was a call to reason, pointing out the insanity of the war and the damage it was doing to science. It attacked blind patriotism, showed the real causes of the war, and called for an international community of nations as a means of ending war.

Although Einstein had little understanding of—and less interest in—politics, he must have known what an uproar this document would cause. It was one thing to be opposed to war in the quiet of the Kaiser Wilhelm Institute, but to do it publicly was to invite attack. It was a measure of his courage that he refused to be silent on such an important matter.

And he did more. In 1915, he went to Switzerland and met the French writer and pacifist Romain Rolland. They had long talks about the causes of the war and how to prevent future war. Rolland was surprised to learn how bitter Einstein was against the "Prussians" and how much he blamed Germany for the war. These visits soon became known, and the attacks on the "Swiss Jew" increased.

The First World War marked the beginning of Albert Einstein's deep involvement in international affairs. His hatred of war would become an obsession. His call for an organization of nations to abolish the insanity of war would never cease. His interest in economics, the wealth of nations, came from his belief that it was a root of the struggle between nations. Gradually he was converted to socialism as the best system for avoiding the competition that led to war.

Despite all these public activities, Einstein was still hard at work on his science. He had constantly in mind the problem of extending special relativity, and he could not let go. It was almost as though there were two men: the fighter against war and the seeker for truth. Or perhaps they were one—the man who thought the search for scientific truth was the finest activity for a man, and killing his fellowman the worst.

Einstein was physically strong, capable of long hours of intense work, but there was a limit. As the war went on, the losses reached several million, the hatred became stronger, and Einstein became ill. It was another attack of the stomach trouble that would plague him all his life. Separated from his family, he was alone in his illness.

Living in Berlin at that time was his father's cousin, Rudolf Einstein, whose wife was Albert's aunt (his mother's sister). Their daughter, Elsa, was a childhood playmate of Albert's from Munich, and it was she who nursed Einstein through his illness in 1917. Cousin Elsa was a plain, nearsighted, kind young woman, recently divorced, with two teenaged daughters. She was totally ignorant of physics and quite impressed by her cousin Albert's fame. They became very good friends and later more than friends.

The problem that he was struggling with now was extending the special theory of relativity. It was a "special theory" because it applied only to observers moving in a straight line at a constant speed. But what was so special about this type of motion? Einstein's intuition told him that relative uniform motion should not be so different from all other motions. What happens if the relative speed changes, say, increases or decreases? What happens to yardsticks and clocks if the straight line becomes a curve?

Then came another brilliant "thought experiment." Think of a woman in a room with no windows. The room is far out in space where there is no gravity. If the woman tries to drop a ball, it will stay where she releases it for there is no gravity to pull it to the floor. But suppose the room is suddenly jerked upward without the woman knowing it. Then the floor will come up and meet the ball. The woman is standing on the floor, so she has been jerked up too. As far as she is concerned, the ball has dropped to the floor! In other words, she is suddenly in a gravity field (see Appendix D).

What is also strange is that a light beam going from one wall to the other would curve downward when the room rises during its passage. So, Einstein said, changing speed (acceleration) has the same effect as gravity. The same thing is true if the room moved at a constant speed, but on a curve and not a straight line.

Now came the mathematics to find out what all this meant. Einstein was not a brilliant mathematician. Many people thought he was because they did not understand how simple the mathematics in the special theory really is. Had he decided to study mathematics rather than physics, Einstein could probably have been outstanding in that field. But mathematics was broken up into dozens of different parts, each of which could take a lifetime's study. Einstein found physics more attractive because it was more unified. When he started to work on his new theory, he had to learn an advanced type of mathematics and often consult mathematicians. It was very hard and there were many false starts, but he had the problem in his mind and he would not let go.

In what kind of space is gravity identical to a change in speed of a body or its moving in a curve? That was the problem that Einstein tackled, and it took him ten years to find the answer. The space is curved!

You may well wonder what a curved space is. Until the general theory of relativity was published, it had always been assumed that space was "flat." By that, we mean that all the axioms of plane geometry as given by Euclid were true. Two parallel lines never meet. The sum of the interior angles of a triangle is exactly 180 degrees. Mathematicians knew that there were other theoretical spaces, some curved like the surface of a sphere, but almost everyone believed that real space and the world we lived in was "flat." In honor of the ancient Greek mathematician, they said the world was "Euclidean."

No, Einstein said, it is flat only when there is no massive body around. Otherwise, the body distorts the space and the space is curved near the body. Newton was wrong. Gravity is not the unexplained attraction between two masses. It is not "action-at-a-distance" that works without any lapse of time. That is impossible. A planet moves like a marble rolling down the rim of a soup bowl. And the soup bowl is just the curved space caused by a large mass of the sun at the bottom. So space is not Euclidean except when there are no large bodies nearby.

The planets move around the sun because the sun's mass has curved the space in which the planets move. They move in an ellipse because that is the shortest distance and takes the least time to make one orbit in curved space-time. Farther from the sun, the curvature of space-time is less and the outer planets move in this reduced curvature.

Any theory must be tested by experiment. Einstein knew that was the only way his new general theory would be accepted by colleagues who were still skeptical about the special theory. Hard work enabled him to find three possible observations to test his work.

Astronomers had known for years of the strange behavior of the planet Mercury. In its ellipse about the sun, Mercury never came back to the same point at which it had started. If we check its closest approach to the sun, we find this point moves along the orbit (see Appendix D) after each revolution. It is a very small shift, but unexplained by Newton's theory of gravity. Since Mercury is the planet closest to the sun, Einstein knew that it should be affected by the curvature of space due to the sun's mass. He calculated what the effect should be on the orbit of Mercury. It was exactly the unexplained amount! The shift was very small; it would take three millions years for the shift to make one complete revolution about Mercury's orbit. And yet it could be understood by applying the laws of general relativity. This was a scientific triumph of the first order.

The second prediction was that light traveling great distances would lose energy and become "redder." This red shift could not be checked in 1916. Over fifty years later, physicists at Harvard University let light fall straight down from the third floor to the basement of the physics building. With very sensitive detectors, they measured the red shift and found it agreed with Einstein's prediction.

The third experimental check was to prove the most dramatic of all. Knowing that light has mass, Einstein found that starlight passing near the rim of the sun should be deflected toward the sun. This again is a very small effect. The angle through which the starlight is deflected is the angle the width of this book would show at a distance of 10 miles (16 km)!

What sort of experiment could show such a small deflection in the blinding light of the sun? Einstein showed how it could be done. During a total eclipse of the sun, he wrote, the stars in the background appear. If we take photographs of these stars during a total eclipse and then later when the sun is not present, the stars close to the rim of the sun will appear to have shifted by this small amount.

Actually, this effect had been predicted by Einstein in

1912 from his first work on the general theory. In fact, a German expedition had gone to the south of Russia in the summer of 1914 to observe a total eclipse of the sun and to take photographs of the stars. But the war broke out, and the scientists became Russian prisoners.

In 1916, with fierce battles raging on all fronts, there was no hope that the German government would pay for another expedition. What did this scientific nonsense have to do with winning the war? It seemed that Einstein would have to wait for a long time before his prediction could be checked (which was lucky for him, since he had made a mistake in arithmetic and had the wrong value for the angle).

But even in the midst of this terrible war, the urge to know the scientific truth had not died out everywhere. Through neutral Holland, the English astronomer Arthur Eddington received a copy of Einstein's paper on general relativity. He immediately recognized its importance and was impressed by the explanation of the shift in the orbit of Mercury. He wanted to do something about checking the deflection of starlight near the sun, but a study of old eclipse photographs proved nothing. What could be done?

Eddington knew that in three years there would be a total eclipse of the sun at a time when it would be in the field of very bright stars. This was a chance to check Einstein's prediction, an opportunity that would not come again for centuries. It must not be missed. Even with the outcome of the war in doubt, the English astronomers began planning their expedition.

The eclipse was due May 29, 1919, and the only land areas where it would be visible were in South America and Africa. Teams would be sent to both spots early enough to take photographs of the stars when the sun was absent. To the English scientists, Einstein was a German and an enemy working in Berlin. But scientific truth was more important than national pride and prestige. They had to know if Einstein was right or wrong.

The war ended in November 1918, and two months later the English teams were at work in northern Brazil and on Prin-

cipe Island in the Gulf of Guinea. They photographed the stars, set up and checked their cameras, and waited for the eclipse.

On the morning of May 29, 1919, it rained heavily at the African site. The team almost lost hope that the eclipse would be seen. Then, about noon, the rains stopped and the skies began to clear. There were still many clouds, but as the moon crossed the disk of the sun, many stars could be seen through the gaps. Feverishly, the scientists made their photographs, working against time.

The results of this expedition were not known immediately. Looking for such a small deflection was slow, painstaking work, and no one wanted to make a mistake. The photographs from the two widely separated teams had to be brought together and compared. It was months before they were certain of the answer.

Einstein was right! Starlight was deflected in passing near the sun and by almost the exact amount that he had predicted. The shift in the orbit of Mercury had been known long before Einstein, but this was startling proof of the general theory. The excitement that followed the publication of the results of the English expeditions was indescribable.

Only Einstein was unmoved. He had known what the answer had to be. If there had been any other result, he would have blamed the difficulties of the experiment and waited for

*Einstein with H. A.
Lorentz (center),
who was one of his
leading supporters,
and Arthur Eddington,
who led the team
of astronomers that
confirmed Einstein's
general theory of
relativity.*

a later test to confirm his prediction. This is not arrogance; this is the self-confidence of genius.

When the telegram arrived with the news of the English confirmation of his theory, riots against the government were occurring in Berlin. Unmoved by the turmoil in the streets, Einstein read the telegram, then handed it to a student. "Here," he said, "perhaps this will interest you."

The war was over. Sickened by the useless slaughter, the people of the warring nations turned from incompetent generals to a new hero. That he was a shy, absentminded professor whose work was far beyond them did not matter. They had been told that he had drawn a new picture of nature and the structure of the universe. Tired of the old, bloody world, they were ready to worship the new one and its creator. For Albert Einstein, it was sudden, overwhelming fame.

It took him a while to realize what was happening. In February, when the English teams were beginning their work, he had arranged a divorce by mutual consent with his wife, Mileva. He agreed to support his family and to give them the money from the Nobel Prize that he was certain would soon be his. Five months later, he married his cousin Elsa. She would be the caring wife that he needed. Now he could go back in peace to his work.

As fame and honors descended on him, Albert Einstein did not rest on his laurels. He would be active and publish good work for another thirty-five years. He would be best known for his relativity theories, but his work on photons and quantum theory were vital contributions to the new physics.

THE EINSTEIN REVOLUTION

6

With the proof of the deflection of starlight, the Einstein revolution burst on the world like a bombshell. Although the mathematical details could be grasped only by a few, the tremendous publicity made it clear to the man in the street that a new scientific age had been born. All our ideas about the universe and man's role in it had been changed almost overnight by the "absentminded professor." The name of Einstein rang around the world.

The biggest impact, of course, was in science—especially physics. Everything was "relative," people said. They did not really understand what that meant, but it had a nice sound to it.

To scientists, the meaning of the two theories of relativity was clearer. The speed of light was a constant no matter how fast the source was moving. All other observations depended on the relative motion of the observer. Space and time were not independent but were one space-time: What one observer measured in another observer's reference system depended on their relative motion. Only the speed of light was the same for the two observers. The effects of relativity were very small at ordinary speeds, where Newton's laws could be used with high accuracy.

The general theory of relativity removed the need for the observers to be moving in a straight line at a constant relative speed. Gravity was now identical with a changing relative speed (acceleration). Massive bodies like the sun distorted space-time near them. The planets, the stars, and the galaxies all moved in this curved space-time in the shortest possible paths. Newton's pull of gravity was no longer needed to explain how the universe operated.

Einstein's relativity was the beginning of a new age in the study of the universe, a study called "cosmology." With this new way of looking at the motion of the heavenly bodies, people started to wonder about the shape of the universe. There were many guesses as to whether it was bounded or unbounded. Was it expanding or not? Was all matter in the form of the star islands we call galaxies evenly distributed through space? All these questions are still being investigated using Einstein's general relativity theory. Unfortunately, the solutions are very difficult to find because of the complicated mathematics, so the questions are still unanswered. Many models of the universe have been suggested, but none proven.

One of the questions that philosophers try to answer is: How do we know what is real? Is this book you are holding a real object or do you just imagine it is? Relativity theory said that the size of the book and the time that it is being read is different for you and for someone moving across the room. And altogether different for someone driving by in a car. What is real about a book if people in relative motion all see if differently? This is just one of the problems that relativity raised for philosophers.

Where is God in Einstein's universe, the religious leaders worried. What are we to say about Creation? Einstein himself was not too concerned about this. He told people that his God existed because of the wonderful order and harmony we see in the world. What is amazing, Einstein believed, is that we can find out so much about the universe. Man is puny but see how much he can learn about the designs of "the Old

Gentleman.'' If you want to wonder, he said, wonder why mathematics can tell us so much about the laws of nature. After all, God created the integers—one, two, three, etc.— but man created all the rest of mathematics. And yet with this tool that he made himself, he is able to probe the structure of the universe and discover nature's laws.

Einstein never doubted that one day we would know the great design of the universe. It might turn out to be bounded or unbounded. It might be forever expanding, fixed, or even shrinking. The galaxies might be evenly scattered through this vast space or clumped together. It did not matter—one day we would know. Relativity was only the first big step.

Einstein's fame with the public rested on relativity, but scientists knew how important his other discoveries were. In 1920, the $E = mc^2$ formula was unproven, but photons, the proof that atoms exist, the photoelectric-effect explanation, and other work all proved him a great leader in physics. He had even done some work that would lead years later to the discovery of the laser!

It is hard to imagine the wave of publicity and admiration that overwhelmed Einstein beginning in 1920. Something about him captured the imagination of a war-weary public looking for new heroes. Relativity was on everyone's tongue. Few understood what it was and what it meant for our ideas of the universe, but it had a magical ring. Newspapers and magazines poured out millions of words, most of them giving a popular but incorrect explanation. Reporters begged for interviews, which Einstein politely declined. Cartoonists loved the absentminded professor with his wild head of hair and childish manner. Huge crowds attended lectures on relativity. Scholars both praised and denounced the new theory.

He disliked being a world-famous figure. They were treating him as if he were a new wonder in a zoo and expecting him to perform. All he wanted was to be left alone to go on with his work, but the world would not allow it. Except for his colleagues—and not all of them—few understood what relativity meant. That did not stop the man in the street from believing that Einstein had changed his life. He was treated like a combination of wizard, movie star, and rock hero.

Sometimes the publicity was ridiculous. There was even a popular song about the man who "attracted some attention when he found the fourth dimension." There were jokes about a man who "went out one night at a speed greater than light, and came back the previous day."

They wrote limericks linking his name with those of two other well-known figures: Gertrude Stein, the avant-garde poet, and Jacob Epstein, the sculptor of distorted modern statues:

> There are three people named Stein.
> There's Gert and there's Ep and there's Ein.
> Gert's poems are punk,
> Ep's statues are junk,
> And nobody understands Ein.

Everything Einstein said was printed on the front pages of newspapers around the world. He used this new power to promote his ideals of an end to war, cooperation between nations, and Zionism—a homeland for the Jewish people. When the League of Nations—the forerunner of the United Nations—was formed, Einstein became a member of a committee to encourage close ties among scientists. Remembering how many scientists had eagerly supported the war, he was not hopeful for the success of this work, but he tried.

He traveled to England and France to lecture and to plead for international cooperation. With the war just ended and passions against Germany still high, it was a courageous thing for him to do. There were protests and angry articles in some newspapers. Pressure was applied to keep the Royal Astronomical Society of England from awarding its Gold Medal to Einstein (he received it six years later).

Another nation that had fought against Germany, the United States, invited him to speak. He went early in 1921 and was received with honor. Universities showered him with honorary degrees, and his lectures were crowded with eager listeners.

On his visit to the United States in 1921,
Einstein and his wife, Elsa, rode in a motorcade
through the streets of New York City.

*In Japan, Albert and Elsa Einstein were
honored with a traditional tea ceremony.*

He went to Japan and was delighted with the charm of the country and the politeness of the people. Everywhere he was treated like visiting royalty and everywhere he acted in the same shy, withdrawn, simple manner. He never grasped the reason for his fame and was bewildered that his work should attract such attention outside scientific circles.

Just before landing in Japan, he was told that he had finally been given the Nobel Prize. However, the Swedish committee had not given him the prize for his work on relativity. Perhaps they were afraid of the quarrels that still raged among scientists about shrinking yardsticks, slow clocks, and curved space. In any case, the prize was given for all of Einstein's work, but only the photoelectric effect was mentioned.

But along with the world fame and praise came bitter attacks from Germans who hated not only relativity but its discoverer. The military defeat of Germany in the First World War led many so-called patriots to blame their country's humiliation on pacifists and Jews. Einstein was both, and had made no secret of his opposition to the war or his Jewish origin. His relativity theory was sneered at as being "Jewish physics" and contrary to the "Aryan spirit of Teutonic man."

Large meetings were held in Berlin in the 1920s to denounce what was called an attack on the German race and its superiority. Philipp Lenard, who had won the Nobel Prize in 1905 for his experiments on the photoelectric effect, was one of the leaders of these attacks on Einstein. In the beginning, he had been a great admirer of Einstein's work and of the man, but he changed after the war. Now he stood before large audiences and denounced relativity as a sham. Because of his prestige as a scientist, he was listened to. And there were others just as famous who spoke and wrote against "Jewish physics."

Einstein's friends defended him and his work. "Even if it should turn out that relativity is not true," they said, "Einstein has done much more and must be considered one of the greatest physicists of our time." Einstein himself attended one of the public meetings and listened with a smile as relativity was denounced as non-German science, a fraud, and an insult to Aryan physics. He refused to be cowed by the tide of attacks. He recognized the "Prussian" mind behind this refusal to accept his work.

In spite of the venom spilled on him, Einstein had hopes for the new Germany that had come out of the war. When the kaiser fled his throne in 1918 and a republic was declared, there was a feeling that democracy had finally come to Germany. To show his support for the new spirit in his homeland, Einstein applied for German citizenship, and it was granted to him. He still kept his Swiss passport, for this type of dual allegiance was allowed in those days. Later, Einstein would call this generous gesture of returning to German citizenship "the worst folly of my life."

Democracy was weak and the "Prussian" spirit strong in the new Germany. In Munich, in the streets Einstein had walked as a boy, a rabble-rouser named Adolf Hitler was appealing to the worst instincts of the German people. He was finding supporters everywhere, Lenard and other scientists among them. Soon the tiny Nazi party would be a major political force. The "patriots" who hated Einstein and his relativity would flock to it.

So violent were those days in Germany that for a time Einstein's friends feared that he might be assassinated. This was not an idle fear, for several officials of the new republic were shot down by "patriots" in the 1920s. For a short time, Einstein canceled all his public lectures and stayed home, but not for long. He appeared boldly at an antiwar meeting and spoke out for pacifism. His enemies were furious, but Einstein would not let them silence him.

Attacked in his own country and wildly praised almost everywhere else in the world—it was a strange life.

But science does not stop its progress for the affairs of men and nations. Einstein's relativity and his photon theory had opened new territories for physicists to explore, and eagerly they rushed in to mine the gold.

In Paris, there were two physicists, brothers. One was a duke and one was a prince, and both were outstanding scientists. Maurice de Broglie (the duke) had been secretary of the Solvay Conference in 1911. When he returned to Paris, he told his younger brother Louis (the prince), about Einstein's amazing ideas that light was a stream of particles called "photons." All through the war, while he worked on improving radios, Prince Louis de Broglie thought deeply about the strange nature of light. How could it be both a wave and a particle? After the war, he started work on the problem in earnest for his Ph.D. thesis.

By 1923, he had an answer. Light was a stream of particles as Einstein had predicted, but each particle was accompanied by a wave that "guided" it. Thus it was not a choice between either waves or particles. Light consisted of both, and one could not be found without the other. This was weird enough, but even stranger was de Broglie's idea that this wave-plus-particle nature was also true of electrons, protons, and every other body!

At first, de Broglie's ideas were ignored. It was contrary to common sense, almost as outrageous as relativity. It was Einstein who recognized that the young French nobleman had made a most important discovery. It was Einstein who brought it to the attention of the scientific world and insisted that it marked the beginning of a new age in understanding matter, atoms, and the nucleus. He pushed the new ideas and put his whole prestige behind them. Being Einstein and at the height of his fame, he had to be listened to. De Broglie's strange explanation was soon on everyone's lips.

No one could predict where such ideas would lead. Even an Einstein could not have guessed what would come from the wave-particle picture.

Soon other men would build on these new ideas. From their research, a new picture of the atom and the nucleus would appear. It would be a world in which nothing was certain, only chance would rule; a "quantum world" obeying quantum laws, a world in which Albert Einstein was one of the first explorers, but which he could never fully accept.

ATTACKING THE QUANTUM WORLD

7

Actually, it was Max Planck who first sighted and named the quantum world back in 1900. The stream of light particles that he called "quanta" (the singular is "quantum") was too strange for him. Even when Einstein showed that these light quanta (which he called "photons") explained the photo-electric effect, Planck could still not believe in their reality. He spent many years trying to prove that the quantum world did not exist—and failed.

After Planck and Einstein came a Danish physicist, Niels Bohr. In 1913, Bohr used quantum ideas to build a new model of the atom. In this picture, electrons circle the nucleus in certain allowed orbits like planets circling the sun. When an electron moved from an outer orbit to an inner one, it gave up energy in the form of light. The problem was that circling electrons should constantly radiate energy and finally fall into the nucleus. So Bohr's model was incomplete.

The puzzle about waves and particles was on everyone's mind. How could light, electrons, protons, and other parts of the nucleus act like a wave sometimes and like a tiny solid body at other times? Did not things have to be one or the other? De Broglie's particle guided by a wave was strange enough, but this answer did not satisfy scientists. What was going on in the quantum world?

The next group of explorers of this invisible world landed on its shores in 1925 and 1926. The first was a twenty-three-year-old German named Werner Heisenberg. He had been studying the problem for several years and had almost given up. Heisenberg suffered from hay fever and in the summer of 1925, he went to an island in the North Sea for relief. Walking the beaches one day, the answer came to him in a flash.

"We can't see atoms," he said to himself. "The quantum world is forever invisible to us. We throw things into it—light, electrons, protons—at high speed and we examine what comes out. One thing that comes out is a bunch of photons of different colors (the spectral lines). Like fingerprints, these are different for different atoms. What we need is some way to predict these lines."

He went back to his cottage and started to work. Soon he had a way of calculating what the spectral lines should be. The mathematics was very weird, but it worked.

At the same time, an Austrian physicist named Erwin Schrodinger had arrived at the same result by a different method. "It is not a particle guided by a wave as de Broglie said," Schrodinger reasoned. "The particle is made up of many waves that cancel each other out except where the particle is." His mathematics was very different from Heisenberg's, but soon it was proven that they were just two different ways of looking at the same thing. And they always gave the same result. This new theory was called "wave or quantum mechanics."

Young people are bold explorers. Aided by a twenty-three-year-old Englishman, Paul Dirac, the new wave mechanics quickly grew into a powerful system for investigating the quantum world. It explained why Bohr's model of the atom worked and its limits. The new theory allowed the spectral lines to be calculated, and much, much more. In a short time, it proved to be one of the most successful theories ever proposed.

But it still did not explain the strange wave and particle behavior of atoms. What were these waves that Schrodinger said added together to form the particle? Were they real like sound and water waves, or even light waves? If they were, how could they be detected? What sort of experiment would trap them and prove they existed?

The answer to these questions was to shatter the old physics even more than did relativity and Planck's light quanta. It was so outrageous that it began a battle that continues even today. On one side were the first explorers of the quantum world: Einstein and Planck; on the other side, the bold young men who were throwing overboard the last bits of Newton's great discoveries. It would be a bitter fight.

The answer was given by a German named Max Born who was Heisenberg's teacher. "These are not real waves," he said. "One can no longer say that at a given moment a particle is at this spot or that. These are waves of probability! With them we can calculate the probability that the particle is at a certain point. But it can be anywhere! The probability will be highest where we would have calculated it was by Newton's rules and small elsewhere. There is no longer any certainty about where a particle is. All we have to work with are the odds on finding it here or there."

This was a stunning conclusion and immediately the older men protested. "There were certain things that Newton had said that could not be questioned. If we know the position and speed of a particle at one time, we can calculate its future path at any later time—Newton said that and it's true. If Born is correct, all we can ever calculate is a bunch of probabilities of its future path. This is crazy."

It may have been crazy, but it worked. "Look," the young rebels said, "the only thing that makes a theory right or wrong is how well it explains experiments. The wave mechanics does that beautifully."

Then Heisenberg struck another blow at the old physics. "In the quantum world," he argued, "you can't know both the position and the speed of a particle at the same time! There will always be a small uncertainty in one or the other. The more precisely you know where the electron or proton is, the less you know of its speed and direction.''

This law he called the ''uncertainty principle.'' It is even crazier than probability waves—and today we know it is just as true.

Niels Bohr brought some order into the confusion that these new wild ideas had brought into physics. He was a brilliant philosopher as well as a great scientist, and he had thought deeply about the meaning of wave mechanics.

Very simply, what he said was this: We live in a world that is forever separated from the quantum world. Ours is a non-quantum world, in part classical and Newtonian. We cannot draw pictures of what goes on in atoms. We cannot even think of things in the quantum world in terms of familiar objects in our nonquantum world—like solid particles and sound waves. To describe what goes on in the quantum world, we must talk of *particles and waves at the same time,* for they are both necessary to describe an electron, for example.

In other words, waves and particles ''complement'' each other, and both are needed to understand the inhabitants of the quantum world. It is as if two blindfolded men are handed a pencil. One grasps it by the eraser and says, ''It is soft and can be bent.'' ''No,'' says the other, ''it's like a hard rod with a sharp point.'' Which one is right? Are they both right, or are they both wrong? Neither, Bohr would say. They must use both descriptions to get an idea of what a pencil is. And if you want to describe an electron, you must use both the wave description and the particle description.

Einstein stood firm against the new wave mechanics. He did not believe it for a minute. He had supported de Broglie with his real particle guided by a wave, but this was too much. Probability instead of certainty, never to know both the exact position and the exact speed of a particle, something that was a wave on one day and a particle on the next. All this revolted him. His intuition and insight told him it had to be wrong. The new wave mechanics, in spite of all its successes, had to be incomplete, like Bohr's old model. Soon, a better

Einstein shares a relaxed moment with Danish physicist Niels Bohr, whose theories of the "quantum world" Einstein could never accept.

theory would come along to wash it away and restore Newton's certainty. Even wrong theories, Einstein pointed out, can give correct answers for a while. Newton, himself, had done wonders in astronomy with the wrong picture of gravity and how it worked.

Einstein would never accept a world built on probability and uncertainty. "God," he said, "does not play dice with the universe." Einstein's God—the God he called "the Old Gentleman"—was too subtle and too good a mathematician to use chance to determine where every nuclear particle in the universe should be an instant later. The instinct that had served Einstein so well in the past told him that this could not be.

The battle for and against the new wave mechanics was fought at dozens of meetings. At the 1927 Solvay Conference, a picture was taken of the scientists. Planck and Einstein are sitting in the front row with the older men. Standing in the back are the young challengers: Bohr, Heisenberg, Schrodinger, and Dirac. Everyone looked very serious. They were about to lock horns on the most vital question of the day. They knew it would determine the future of physics for years to come.

It always started the same way. Einstein would stand up and propose a "thought experiment" which he claimed showed that probability waves did not exist or that the uncertainty principle was wrong. These were always very clever schemes, well thought out, and always simple to grasp. At first it would appear that Einstein was triumphant, that he had really found a flaw that proved his point. But time and again, Bohr would find the mistake in Einstein's reasoning. It was not easy. Battling with an Einstein was no job for anyone but a Bohr. Once, the Dane spent a sleepless night walking up and down in his hotel room, before he found the answer. This time he was able to show that Einstein had forgotten his own general theory of relativity. The "thought experiment," Bohr proved, was really a clever way to show that the uncertainty principle was correct!

Undaunted, Einstein came back time and time again with

new ways of attacking wave mechanics. He believed in his intuition, and that intuition told him Bohr's interpretation had to be wrong. It was all in vain, Bohr knocked down every objection, and in the meantime, the new theory went on to greater and greater success. Dirac even made it agree with relativity. He predicted that there was a new particle as light as the electron but with a positive charge. It was soon found.

Einstein was not alone in his fight against probability and uncertainty. Planck was unhappy with it, and later even Schrodinger began to have his doubts. But it was Einstein who was in the forefront of the fight. Like the old Saxon king, Canute, he stood at the water's edge and ordered the tide to go back. And the tide overwhelmed him.

Einstein's attitude bewildered his friends and colleagues. What had happened to the rebel, the leader, the man who had so boldly planted his flag on the beaches of the quantum world? Now he was acting like the old fogies who just would not believe in relativity or photons or even atoms. Had he grown old and therefore conservative? But he was not even fifty years old yet.

It saddened people to see Einstein stubbornly refuse to accept the new wave mechanics. They knew he was fighting a losing battle. Instead of leading them into deeper explorations of the quantum world, he was wasting his time and energy on futile quarrels about the equipment. "Well," the scientists said, "if he won't lead us, too bad. We still have Bohr, and he knows the way."

His friends knew that Einstein was not well, and they worried about his health. In 1928, he was found to have a serious heart condition and was warned to take it easy. He refused to stop working, for physics was his life. Death did not frighten him. The idea of a world ruled by uncertainty and chance— that bothered him.

The celebration of his fiftieth birthday was a world event. Cables and telegrams poured in, and the newspapers printed millions of words about him. Einstein never liked this sort of fame, and he spent the day hiding from well-wishers.

He was absorbed in finding new flaws in Bohr's arguments, but found time for world affairs. He wrote about the financial crisis brought on by the crash of the stock market in the United States. The worldwide depression that followed brought widespread unemployment and misery to Germany and many other nations. But in Germany, these events would lead to different consequences. As Albert Einstein worked in his quiet study in Berlin, dark clouds were gathering over Europe.

In January 1933, Adolf Hitler. came to power as chancellor (prime minister) of Germany. It was the beginning of a return to the dark ages. Hitler's Nazi party began immediately to seize control, using terror to crush their foes. They had long proclaimed their ideas about the superiority of the Teutonic race, the Aryan man. Now they put these ideas into practice in the bloodiest possible way. The opponents they did not kill, they threw into concentration camps. Freedom of speech vanished. Democracy was sneered at Books that promoted these "non-Aryan" ideas were thrown into heaps and publicly burned. Nazi Germany began to rearm and prepare for war against the "weak" democracies.

Einstein had been lecturing at the California Institute of Technology when Hitler came to power. The Jewish pacifist knew that his fame would not save him from the Nazi terror. No one was more hated by the German "patriots" than the man of peace. Not only were the Nazis violently anti-Jewish, but they had led the fight against relativity and "Jewish physics." Also they had never forgiven Einstein for preaching against war and accepting German citizenship under the republic. He was a marked man, high on the lists of the Nazi secret police.

Einstein could not go back to Berlin. Where then? For years now, all the universities outside of Germany had tried to attract him with generous offers. He had refused all these, politely but firmly. He felt that he was too old to pull up roots and leave. In order to teach in another country, he would have to learn the language, and Einstein felt comfortable only when speaking German.

But now the Nazis had made the decision for him. Other Jewish scientists were fleeing Germany after losing their jobs. For Einstein to return to Berlin was out of the question. His life would be in real danger from his enemies.

For over a year, a very attractive offer had been sitting on Einstein's desk. It came from a brand-new research facility, the Institute for Advanced Studies, in Princeton, New Jersey. It offered Einstein freedom to do exactly as he wished. He could spend all his time doing his research and, once a year, give a lecture to his colleagues on his progress. Einstein had been asked to name his own salary. The number he picked was so low that the shocked institute officials tripled it. It was a hard offer to turn down. In Princeton, Einstein knew, he would be safe from the Nazis.

It was a difficult decision. Leaving Europe and all his old friends and colleagues would be a wrenching experience. Should he think of his own safety when these same friends were in danger? Could he fight the Nazis better from Europe or the United States? From his lecture trip to California, Einstein went back to Europe—not to Berlin, but to a seaside resort in Belgium. The king and queen of Belgium were good friends, and they sent bodyguards to protect him. Yet Einstein walked the beaches alone and tried to make up his mind. This was not the type of question he was used to considering.

The Nazis had no doubts about what they wanted to do. Three months after they came to power, they decided to move against Einstein. First, they grabbed his bank account and his home. Learning that Einstein had already declared his intention of dropping his German citizenship, the Nazis quickly revoked it. Planck protested this action, and it was very courageous of him to speak out at that time. An angry Hitler threatened to send Planck to a concentration camp. No one was allowed to say a good word for "the Jew Einstein." Out of fear, many German scientists remained silent.

Einstein resigned from the Kaiser Wilhelm Institute and from the Prussian Academy of Science. To the academy, which had been about to expel him by order of the Nazis, Einstein sent a bitter letter telling them what he thought of their cowardly actions. He told them that they had stood by without a word of protest while the Jewish scientists had been expelled and forced to flee. He would not be a member of any society that had acted in this manner, even if it was under force.

It was clear that Hitler would lead Germany to war. Which was worse: the Nazis or war? Einstein struggled with his conscience about this question and then decided that nothing would be worse than a Nazi Europe. That decision meant a compromise with his lifelong pacifism. Now, he believed that young men should be willing to join their countries' armies to fight against Hitler. It hurt him to say this, but there was no other choice.

From Belgium, the Einsteins went to England. Albert talked to the British leaders about the menace of nazism and warned of the coming war. He also worked hard to help the many Jewish scientists who had fled from Germany. For them, he found money, housing, and jobs. He was available to all. No appeal was ever in vain. These trained minds, he knew, would be important in the war against Hitler.

He also made a decision about his own future. He would take the job in Princeton and continue the fight from there. In October 1933, the Einsteins sailed for the United States. They would never again return to Europe.

EINSTEIN
AND
AMERICA

8

The Einsteins received a warm, almost royal welcome when they landed in the United States. President Roosevelt invited them to the White House, the newspapers covered their every move, and ordinary people lined up for a glimpse of a genius. The public acclaim was not to Einstein's liking. He wanted peace and quiet so he could go on with his work. But the rise of Hitler's Germany would not allow him to retire from the world.

Princeton was a small college town with tree-lined streets dominated by the spreading campus. The townspeople were curious about the newcomer. The legend of the absent-minded, badly dressed thinker who had changed the universe had preceded Einstein. What surprised them was his lack of formality and of stuffiness. They found him gentle, kind, and often lost in his own thoughts. His right to privacy was respected even when he walked the streets alone. Here he had no need for bodyguards.

He bought a house at 112 Mercer Street, a modest two-story structure. There was a lawn, trees and hedges, and a porch. It was close to the institute, where he had his office. He

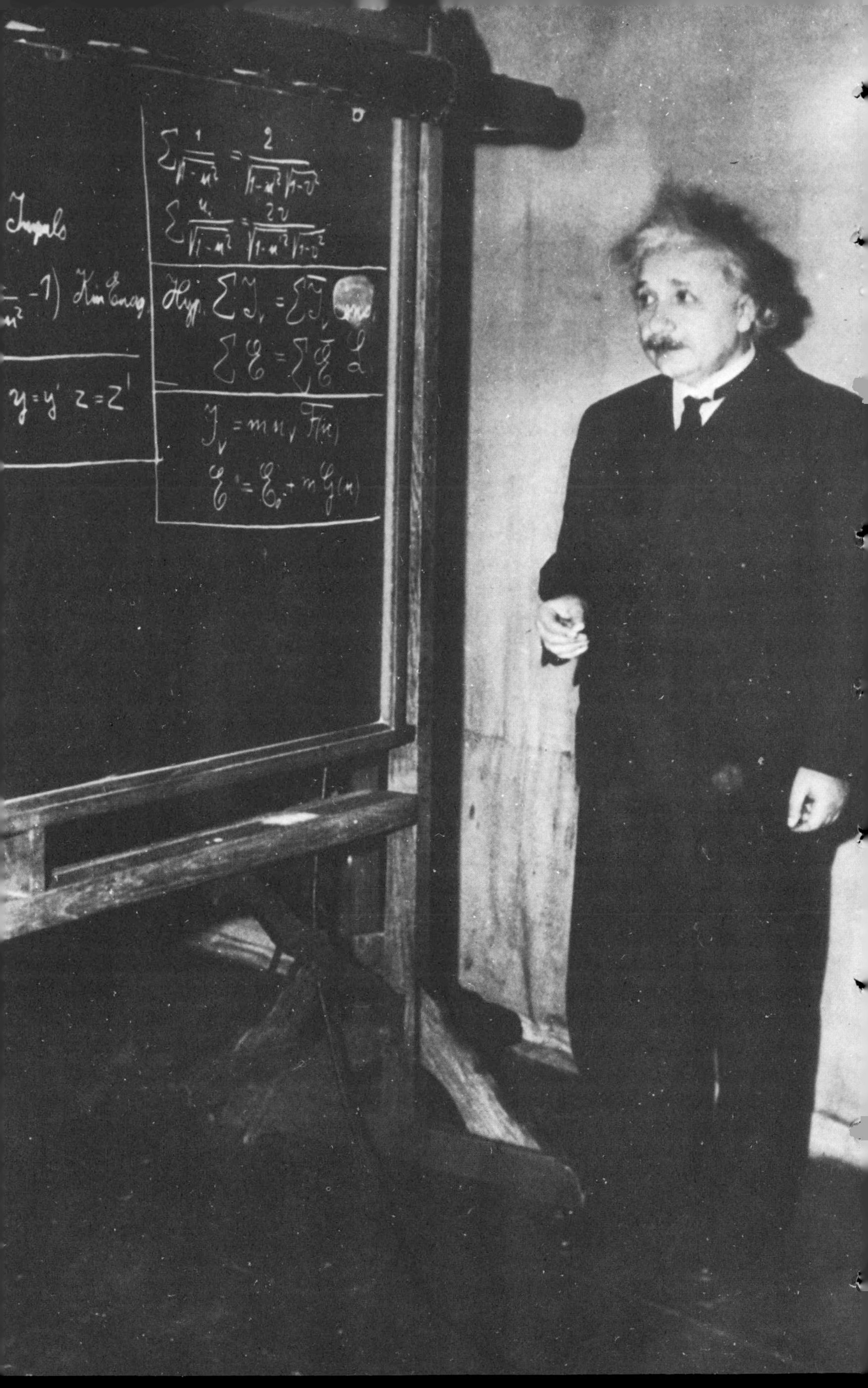
Impuls
Kin Energ.
Hyp.

had a study built on the second floor, filled with books and a desk cluttered with pencils, paper, and pipes. Here he would live and work for the rest of his life.

The quarrel with Bohr over probability and uncertainty went on, but new events were pushing it into the background. A year before his arrival in the United States, a new nuclear particle had been discovered—the neutron. It had the same mass as a proton but no charge. This meant that it was perfect for bombarding other nuclei, which repelled charged particles. In Rome, Enrico Fermi had hit uranium with neutrons and formed a new element called neptunium. It was a very exciting time. All sorts of new discoveries were about to be made.

In Europe, the dark clouds continued to gather. Hitler was rearming and threatening war. Einstein was busy helping the many refugee scientists who had fled Germany and later Austria, when Hitler marched into that country. Warning people about the menace of nazism took time away from his work, but he knew it was vital. There would be no free search for the truth in the world if Hitler won.

In December 1936, Elsa Einstein died after a long illness. Because he had devoted so much time to his work during this time, many people judged Einstein harshly. He was grief-stricken over his wife's death, but he was not a man to show this openly. Besides, he did not think that man's—or woman's—suffering in this world was important. What was important was the search for the scientific truth about that world. His stepdaughter, Margot, and his faithful secretary stepped in to relieve him of the petty concerns of everyday life. They

Shortly after his arrival in the United States, Einstein addressed a conference of the American Association for the Advancement of Science in Pittsburgh, Pennsylvania.

saw to it that he was fed, clothed, and had money in his pocket. Einstein could not be bothered by these time-consuming needs.

Many people thought he was selfish. If he was, it was for his work and not for himself. He was getting older and no longer felt the sharp intuition that had served him so well as a young man. And there was so much research to be done.

As 1938 ended, the newspapers were still full of events in Europe. The leaders of England and France had given in to Hitler over his demands for part of Czechoslovakia. They had signed a pact with the Nazi dictator at Munich, a treaty they hoped meant peace. But betraying the Czechs would not save them from war.

Because of the political turmoil, there was little mention in the newspapers about something that had happened in Berlin that was much, much more important to the future of the world than the Munich Pact. And even if the event had received more attention in the press, no one but the scientists would have understood its world-shaking implications.

At the Kaiser Wilhelm Institute for Chemistry, two German chemists had been bombarding uranium with neutrons to check Fermi's work. Unlike Fermi, they carefully analyzed the material after it had been bombarded. To their surprise, they found that some of the uranium had become two lighter elements! The uranium nuclei had been split by the neutrons. No one had ever dreamed that this was possible.

Being good colleagues, they wrote of this amazing result to Lise Meitner, a former co-worker on the project. Dr. Meitner had been forced to flee to Sweden. As an Austrian Jew, she had been in danger when Hitler occupied her homeland.

Lise Meitner immediately realized what the news meant. If in splitting, the uranium nucleus sent out another neutron, this could split another uranium nucleus—and so on, and so on. The whole thing could build up into a gigantic explosion. From Einstein's formula ($E = mc^2$), the final energy of the explosion could be calculated. A very small amount of uranium could be a bomb equal to thousands of tons of TNT!

Frightened by the idea that the Nazis might soon have such a weapon, Meitner told her nephew, who told Bohr. Soon Bohr was in the United States telling the American scientists about "nuclear fission," the splitting of the uranium nucleus by neutrons. It was clear that an unbelievably powerful explosive could come from this scientific discovery.

In a very short time, experiments proved that indeed the split uranium nucleus did send out more neutrons. Now it was no longer a possibility; it was a fact. Uranium was a great danger and must be kept out of the hands of the Nazis.

Einstein was urged to use his friendship with the queen of Belgium to keep the largest stock of uranium in the world, that in the Belgian Congo, out of Hitler's hands. Then it was decided that it was more urgent that President Roosevelt be warned of the danger. After all, the Germans had captured the uranium mines in Czechoslovakia, where there was enough material to make many nuclear bombs.

It was at the urging of a group of foreign scientists, refugees from Hitler, that Einstein wrote to the American president to warn of the nuclear bomb threat. Einstein's letter, dated August 2, 1939, is famous;

> Sir: Some recent work . . . leads me to expect that the element uranium may be turned into a new and important source of energy in the immediate future . . . it is conceivable . . . that extremely powerful bombs of a new type may . . . be constructed. A single bomb of this type, carried by boat or exploded in a port, might very well destroy the whole port together with some of the surrounding territory. However, such bombs may very well prove too heavy for transportation by air. . . .

The letter went on to point out that the Germans had the Czech uranium mines and competent scientists. It urged that the uranium work in the United States be speeded up and that the government take other steps promptly to meet the threat of a Nazi nuclear bomb.

Thus it was that the man who detested war, the lifelong

pacifist, started the work that would lead to Hiroshima and Nagasaki. Later, when the threat of nuclear war hung over the world, Albert Einstein would suffer deep pain for his role in developing nuclear weapons. But his part in it was nothing more than signing this letter. The atomic bomb would have been made without him. Too many people, American and English, knew about it and knew of the danger of a Nazi bomb. If the letter had never been written, sooner or later, the Manhattan Project would have been formed to build the bomb. However, Einstein's signature started it off early enough to beat the Germans to the goal.

President Roosevelt acted promptly on receiving the letter. Einstein's name at the bottom was good enough for the president to order a Uranium Committee to be formed to push the building of an atomic bomb. Scientists and government officials began work to obtain a sufficient supply of uranium and to push the necessary experimental investigations.

One month later, Hitler invaded Poland and the Second World War began. Now the uranium work was a matter of survival for the democracies. If Hitler got it first, they were doomed.

In March 1940, Einstein sent a second letter to the president. He said that the Germans were carrying out uranium research in great secrecy at the Kaiser Wilhelm Institute. He warned that papers would soon appear in the U.S. scientific journals on how to make a uranium bomb. These, Einstein urged, should not be published and only the government could stop their appearance.

Here Einstein's involvement with the building of the atomic bomb ceases. He wrote two letters but was allowed no other role. He might not have wished to take part, for he had strong doubts that such a bomb could ever be built. Perhaps he wished that it would prove impossible for scientific reasons. His instinct might have told him what the future world would be with nuclear bombs. In any case, the government officials in charge of the uranium work saw that he was not kept informed of the progress being made. Einstein, the ex-pacifist, the socialist, the absentminded professor, could not be trusted to keep military secrets.

Seven years after his arrival in the United States, Albert Einstein took the oath of allegiance and became a citizen of his new homeland. Although he had been born, educated, and had triumphed in Europe, he would never see it again. It was with a twinge of regret that he cut his ties to the past.

The Japanese attacked Pearl Harbor on December 7, 1941, and the war was now truly a world war. Excluded from the atomic bomb work, Einstein was a consultant to the navy on special problems involving explosives of the ordinary kind. He remained in Princeton and did what he could to help defeat Hitler.

For four more years, the battles raged in Europe, Africa, and the Pacific. At first, the Nazis and their Japanese allies were victorious everywhere, but slowly and at great cost, the tide changed. The enemy was being pushed back steadily before the ever-growing power of the Allied armies. By the middle of 1943, it was clear who would win.

The only chance for Hitler would have been getting an atomic bomb before the Americans and British. There was a German project run by Heisenberg to work on the application of nuclear fission. Later, they would deny that they were trying to make a bomb. It was only a source of energy, a new type of steam plant using the heat from splitting of uranium, they would insist. Few would believe them, certainly not Einstein who knew what "Prussians" were capable of. No, it was the wartime shortages, the Allied air raids, and the shortsightedness of the German scientists that saved the Allies. Compared to the tremendous effort in money and manpower that England and the United States devoted to building the atomic bomb, the Nazi effort was puny. Also, Heisenberg and the other top scientists made too many wrong guesses about how it could be done. In July 1945, the first nuclear bomb was successfully tested in New Mexico. By then, Germany was defeated and Hitler had killed himself. But there was still Japan, a nation willing to fight to the death.

When Einstein learned of the dropping of the atomic bomb on Hiroshima, he cried out in pain. He realized what a terrible force had been released in the world. He blamed himself for signing the letter to President Roosevelt. What a terrible proof of his mass-energy equation this was! It had cost 120,000 lives in Hiroshima and Nagasaki.

The war ended with total victory for the Allies. But for Einstein and other scientists, it was a bitter victory because of the atomic bomb. They could see the coming struggle between the United States and the Soviet Union. If world war came now, it would be fought with nuclear weapons and could mean the end of mankind. Although his hope was for a world government, Einstein joined a committee of concerned scientists to work for international control of atomic energy. Only if nations shared the awesome power of the atomic bomb would there be a hope for peace. If only the United States and England had the secret, the Soviet Union would soon develop the bomb and an arms race would begin. The Soviets had top scientists too. It took them three years to build an atomic bomb, and the hope for international cooperation vanished.

Also with the end of the war came the ghastly news of the Holocaust. From the Nazi death camps, the survivors told of the killing of millions of innocent men, women, and children, mostly Jewish. It was a horror that shook the world. Even Einstein never dreamed that Germans were capable of such large-scale murder. His hatred for anything German was overwhelming. After the war, the German academies invited him to be a member again. He refused, denouncing them for their cowardly attitude. "The crime of the Germans is truly the most abominable in the history of the so-called civilized nations," he wrote. Because of the Holocaust, no self-respecting Jew would want to belong to a German academy. This hatred of everything German he would carry to the grave.

His last years were filled with public controversy and private sorrow. He fought against the nuclear arms race and was denounced by "patriots" who feared the Soviets. He stood up against the anti-Communist ranting of Senator Joseph McCarthy and was called an atheist and a red by an angry congressman. For Einstein, who loved peace and the quiet of his study, it was a terrible time. But he fought on for what he belived in. His support was invaluable. The name of Albert Einstein still meant something in the world. His words were listened to. His first wife, Mileva, died in 1948. Einstein was not close to his two sons. The older, Hans Albert, is today a professor of engineering in California. The younger son, Eduard, has been in and out of mental hospitals most of his adult life. Albert's beloved sister, Maja, who had joined him just before the war, suffered a paralyzing stroke and lingered for five years before she died. Einstein had spent long hours reading to her during her illness. Now she was gone, and he felt terribly alone. He was seventy-two years old and a sick man himself. He had had a major operation, and the doctors had found a weak spot in a heart artery. They had warned him to take it easy but he refused. There was still too much to be done. "Death comes to everyone," he said. "It is an old debt that will soon be paid."

Honors still came to him. When the first president of the new state of Israel died, Einstein was offered the largely ceremonial position. Despite his strong support for Israel as the Jewish homeland, he gently declined the honor. He pleaded his lack of experience as a statesman and administrator. "I know something about nature," he said, "but little about people." Now he was a living legend.

The young explorers of the quantum world had made great strides in exploring the atom and the nucleus. In this work, Einstein had no part. His scientific colleagues whispered that he was a "museum piece," far from the mainstream of modern physics. They predicted that the great unified field theory that he had been working on for twenty years would never be finished. Many regretted his stubborn refusal to accept a world of uncertainty, a world in which God threw dice. They wished that he could still be the leader he once was, leading them with his marvelous intuition deeper and deeper into the still uncharted parts of the quantum world. But it was not to be.

He was old now, tired and sick, but undaunted. There was still a twinkle of delight in the brown eyes. He was a familiar sight walking slowly through Princeton from the institute to his home. In the winter, he wore a shabby overcoat, a muffler, and a knit ski cap. In the summer, his usual outfit was an old sweater, baggy pants, and sneakers.

They told funny stories about the "Professor." How a little girl had fed him candy while he did her math homework. How he was always forgetting his address and had to telephone his secretary to get it. How he could never remember where he was supposed to be at a given time and had to be searched for. The little girl never existed, but the story tells of Einstein's genuine humility and simplicity. He never lost the childish curiosity about the world he had shown while playing with the magnetic compass when he was five. He was delighted to see that same curiosity in other children.

That need to know how the world worked kept him at his desk, probing the secrets of nature with pencil and paper. His colleagues may have given up on him, but Einstein did not particularly care. After all, he had proved them wrong many times before. Perhaps before the end, he could prove them wrong once more. If he could, it would be the greatest triumph of his amazing career. The problem he had struggled with for the last twenty years was colossal.

What he was trying to find was a new theory that would explain in one set of equations both gravity and the electromagnetic field. This theory he hoped would come out of a new approach to the general theory of relativity. Now he worked with younger men as assistants, explaining where the problems were, and suggesting how they could be solved. It turned out to be very difficult mathematics, impossible to solve. Without solutions, there could be no experiments to prove it right or wrong. And a new theory is only as good as the experimental proof.

To combine two phenomena like gravity and the electromagnetic field in one set of equations is to unify them, so we call such a theory a "unified field theory." It was to be Einstein's last problem. He had started on his unified field theory in 1920. Now he was in his middle seventies, but the will to know was as strong as ever.

Albert Einstein conducts an informal seminar
at the Institute for Advanced Study in Princeton,
New Jersey, where he spent his final years
attempting to prove his unified field theory.

He worked hard, following the usual dead-ends and false starts. At times he was very discouraged, but he refused to give up. If a man is his work and not his suffering, then if he stops working, he is nothing. It did not matter how famous he was and what marvelous things he had done before. Einstein had dedicated his life to his work and had given up warm personal relationships with people he loved and countless pleasures for it. To stop searching now would be the worst form of betrayal.

Several times he thought he had arrived at the great breakthrough. With great publicity, his papers on the unified field theory appeared in the learned journals. But the disappointing thing was that there were no solutions, no way to find out if it was right or wrong. Once he thought that he could even explain the particulate structure of matter—electrons, protons, and neutrons would appear as solutions of another set of equations. This too was shown to be wrong. Einstein had failed in the biggest search of all.

Still, as one wise scientist pointed out, he was entitled to this failure. He had done more than any other man for the beginnings of the new physics. He had boldly charted the beaches of the quantum world. If he had failed to go into the jungle, well, that was a job for younger men. There were strange creatures in those trees—waves and particles that were the same thing. And uncertainty and probability, so that one could never be sure where the animals were.

In April 1955, Einstein began to suffer from severe stomach pains. The doctors were alarmed and suggested an immediate operation. Einstein refused. He knew it was a long shot for a man his age and probably useless. He had lived with the idea of death for some years now and he was unafraid. It was time for him to pay the "old debt."

Two days after the first attack, he was taken to Princeton Hospital. For a while, it seemed that he might recover, that the weak spot in his heart artery might heal itself.

Shortly after midnight on April 18, 1955, he began to mutter in his sleep. He was talking German, the language in which he was most comfortable. Before the doctors could be called, the weak artery broke and Albert Einstein died. We will never know his last words, for only a nurse was present and she understood no German.

Einstein had been very firm in his instructions: no funeral, no grave, and no monument. His remains were to be cremated. Neither his ashes, his home, nor his office was to become a shrine. A man had died and that was the end of it. If it had been a worthy life, his work would be remembered. All the rest, his pain and suffering, his failures, his regrets, counted for nothing. Only the work was important.

His wishes were carried out to the letter. After cremation, his ashes were hidden. It is thought that later they were secretly thrown into the Delaware River. With his family's approval, Einstein's brain was removed during the autopsy and carefully examined under a microscope. Although nothing has ever been published about this examination, it is known that the doctors found nothing unusual. In size, weight, and formation, it was perfectly normal. Under the microscope, the cells were just what one would expect for a man of seventy-six with Einstein's medical history. It could have been the brain of any elderly man.

Einstein's life was his work, and his work lives on. Scientists are still exploring and expanding different parts of relativity and photon theory. New proofs of the truths that Einstein discovered are being found. A clock in a spacecraft speeding around the earth at high-speed was found to run more slowly than a clock on the earth's surface. In the high-energy collisions of nuclei and in the quasars, neutron stars, and black holes in space, nature seems to follow Einstein's laws.

The latest theory says that the universe began with the "Big Bang." This was a gigantic explosion from which all the planets, stars, and galaxies finally came. We know that the universe is still expanding, but whether this expansion will go on without limit or will reverse, we do not know. Perhaps it will all fall back together and we will have another "Big Bang," and so on without end. The new relativity theories built on Einstein's work may answer that question.

There is still no theory unifying gravity and the electromagnetic field, but it may be coming. At least Einstein's failure to find such a theory showed what should not be tried. Trying new approaches, physicists have succeeded in "unifying" the electromagnetic field and the two nuclear forces that keep protons and neutrons inside the nucleus. This is a triumph not only for relativity but for the quantum theory. Probability and uncertainty have gone from victory to victory in explaining the nuclear world. Today, few scientists challenge their truth.

Newton carried on from Galileo, and Einstein completed the work of Newton. Someday, someone will appear to perfect the work of Albert Einstein. Science never stops when one of its giants dies. It moves forward without halting. It makes mistakes, corrects them, makes theories, discards them, then makes other theories. It is an endless process.

Every hundred years, someone appears to carry science to a new mountaintop. From there, scientists can see the next peak to be scaled. They can see so clearly because "they are standing on the shoulders of giants."

The scientist for our hundred years was Albert Einstein.

APPENDIX A
NEWTON'S
SPACE AND
TIME

Isaac Newton was a scientific genius and a deeply religious man. His work was dedicated to the glory of God. Newton's God had wound up the great clockwork that was the universe. His God had created space and time.

Newton's laws were set in an *absolute space*. It had no boundaries, never moved or changed, and was completely empty. It existed because God was everywhere. Indeed, this absolute space was a proof of the existence of God. Time was also absolute. It flowed without change and always had since the Creation.

All this is good theology but bad physics. Galileo had shown that all motion of particles was "relative." There must be some reference that the particle is moving with respect to (even if that reference is moving relative to another reference!). If you shift this book from one hand to the other, it is moving with respect to the walls and floor of the room (and the room is rotating on an earth that is orbiting a sun that is moving through a galaxy! The path of the moving book depends on the reference system selected, but there must be one). In an empty absolute space, where is the reference for a moving particle?

And what kind of time is absolute time if there is no other clock to compare it with? It was all very strange.

Because of the success of Newton's laws in explaining the motion of the planets, only a few scientists protested that something was wrong with these ideas of space and time. No one else had anything better to offer. It took over a hundred years before some errors started to creep in and people began to wonder again if Newton was right. Until then, everyone believed absolutely in absolute space and time.

Imagine that you are riding on a train that is in uniform motion on a very smooth track (no jolting, no swaying from side to side, no accelerations). Can you tell if you are at absolute rest or in absolute motion? "Sure," you say, "all I have to do is look out the window and see the telegraph poles and everything else whizzing by." Ah, but that is *relative motion*, motion relative to something that you consider fixed, namely, the ground along the track. We have already conceded that *relative* motions can be determined. What we asked is: Can you prove that the ground is at absolute rest? If you can by some ingenious experiment determine this, then absolute space and absolute time make sense, but what if you cannot? Is it not possible that the train is at rest and everything outside is in uniform motion past your window?

Let us go back to the train and find some of the consequences of Newton's mechanics. This time, we will move past a platform on which an observer is standing. Suppose I fire a gun toward the front of the train and measure the speed of the bullet. The observer on the platform also measures the bullet's speed. According to Newton, I find the bullet to be moving at the speed which it had on leaving the muzzle. But the observer outside finds the bullet's speed to be the muzzle velocity *plus* the speed of the train. And if the gun had been fired toward the rear of the train, the observer would have measured the bullet's speed as its muzzle velocity *minus* the train's speed. This is Newton's "addition of velocities" law. (See Fig. 1, p. 103.)

This will surprise no one, for it is just everyday experience and common sense. This is what is meant by Newton's

FIGURE 1

"theory of relativity." It says that the determination of the speed of a moving body depends on the observer's relative motion. It is true only if the relative motion is uniform, i.e., in a straight line at a constant speed. If the speed changes or the train is on a curved track, there is a force acting on the bullet in its flight and none of this applies.

Notice that measuring a speed means measuring a time. According to Newton, the time is the same for both observers. It is not changed by their relative motion.

APPENDIX B
LIGHT WAVES
AND
THE "ETHER"

Trouble for Newton's theory of relativity began with experiments that showed light acting like a wave and not a stream of luminous particles.

It was only in the second half of the nineteenth century that James Clerk Maxwell, a Scottish physicist, discovered what the light wave really was. He took all the known experimental facts about electricity and magnetism and made a theory. Electric currents can be created by a magnet. Magnetism can be created by an electric current. Therefore, Maxwell said, they are really two forms of the same thing: an electromagnetic field. Light was simply an electromagnetic wave. Experiments by Heinrich Hertz proved that this was true.

But if light was a wave then there had to be some medium in which it moved. Sound waves travel through air, and water waves through water, but light traveled through air, water, transparent solids, and even a vacuum! What kind of medium could explain such behavior?

There had to be something there to carry the light waves, so they invented it and called it the "ether." It was a kind of invisible jelly that quivered as it sent light waves on. It filled all space, and massive bodies could move through it without disturbing it. It had to be inside glass, fill a vacuum, and allow the solar system to hurtle through it without any apparent effect. A very strange material indeed.

If an experiment could be done to detect the "ether wind" as the earth passed through it, then the motion of the earth was absolute. The "ether" would be the fixed walls and floor needed to describe the path of a moving body.

The most famous attempt to find the "ether wind" was made between 1881 and 1888 by A. A. Michelson, an American astronomer. He compared the time it took two light beams to travel equal distances. By rotating the apparatus, one beam would be parallel to the "ether wind" and the other perpendicular. The slightest difference in travel time could be seen. It was the same as a swimmer going against, then with, a current and one going from across and back. The first swimmer will always take more time on a round trip.

The result of Michelson's experiment was zero delay. Either there was no "ether" or the "ether wind" did not slow up light. It was suggested by H.A. Lorentz and G.F. Fitzgerald that distances parallel to the "ether wind" shrank just enough to give a zero delay. No one could understand this. Something was seriously wrong with the idea of the "ether".

The problem was that light waves did not obey Newton's relativity. To see why, let's go back to the train and the observer on the platform. The man on the train shines a flashlight forward and then backward and measures the speeds of the two beams, finding they are exactly the speed of light— 186,000 miles (299,000 km) per second. But what about observer B on the platform? According to Newton, B should find the forward beam increased by the speed of the train and the backward beam decreased by the same amount. But Michelson's experiment had shown that this is wrong. There is no "ether wind" to slow down or speed up the light beams. The man on the platform will also measure the speed of the two light beams to be 186,000 miles per second!

Either Maxwell and Michelson were wrong or Newton's relativity did not apply to light waves.

APPENDIX C
THE SPECIAL
THEORY OF
RELATIVITY

Einstein started with two assumptions. Since all experiments to detect the "ether wind" had failed, he postulated (that is, assumed) that the speed of light would be the same for all observers in relative uniform motion. He also assumed that the laws of nature would be the same for these observers.

It was Einstein's genius to recognize that the problem involved our ideas of space and time. Even more remarkable was his intuition that what was involved was what we meant when we say "the two events happened simultaneously, that is at the same instant in time." No one had ever questioned this before. We instinctively feel that we know what simultaneous events are, but Einstein asked the critical question: "How do we know?"

Let's go back to the observer on the platform. Suppose she is a well-trained physicist and is studying simultaneous events. She has erected two poles at opposite ends of the long platform and put a light bulb atop each pole. She carefully finds the exact point at the center of the line between the two poles. The bulbs flash, and the light beams travel to the center point, where our physicist measures their time of arrival with some electronic apparatus (called "coincidence circuits"). So, in this case, she can clearly tell if two events are simultaneous. If the two beams arrive at the center point at the same time, they must have started at the same time, for the speed of light in air is a constant.

But now the train comes rushing past the platform and it carries another well-trained physicist as a passenger. What does she find? Are the two events still simultaneous for an observer in uniform motion with respect to the platform?

We change nothing in this "thought experiment" if we put the observer on the train opposite the center point when the bulbs are flashed. As the light from the bulbs is traveling to the center point, the train (and the observer) moves closer to one pole and farther from the other. (See Fig. 2, p. 109.)

The light from bulb A will reach the woman on the train before the light from bulb B. So, she will say that the two bulbs were *not* flashed at the same time. The woman on the platform will still insist that they were. Who is right? They both are. Events can be simultaneous for one observer and not for another who is in uniform motion relative to the first.

Now you see why no one thought of this before Einstein. The speed of light is much greater than the speed of the train and other everyday speeds. The difference in this case is very, very small. But suppose it was an electron moving almost at the speed of light? Then the difference is important.

Now Einstein did the mathematics which gave the difference in what the two observers saw. It turned out that all measurements that either observer made in the other's space and time depended on the speed of their relative motion. The other observer's yardstick shrank and her clock ran slow because measuring these while moving past them involves measuring simultaneous events.

Suppose a man on the ground is doing the following experiment to determine the length of a yardstick. Standing at one end of the yardstick, he sends a pulse of light to a mirror at the other end. The pulse is reflected back to him, and he measures the round-trip time with great accuracy. Since the

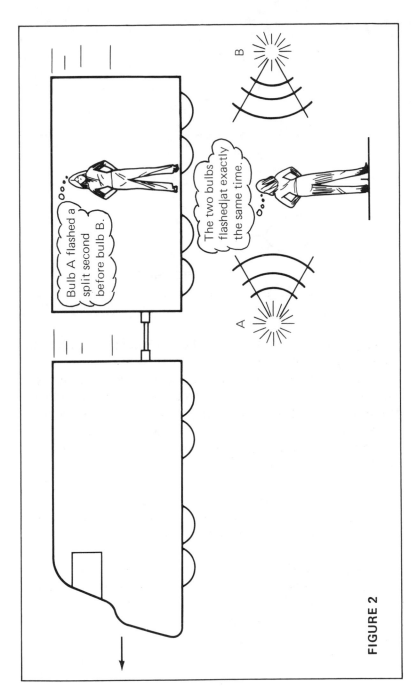

FIGURE 2

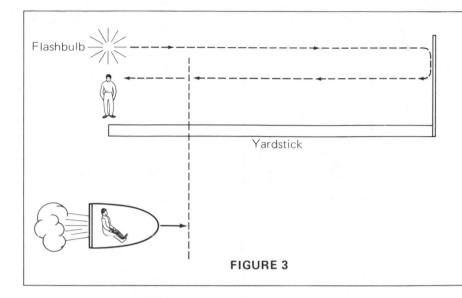

Flashbulb

Yardstick

FIGURE 3

speed of light is constant, a little arithmetic gives him the exact length of the yardstick. (See Fig. 3 above.)

Just as the pulse starts out, a man in a rocket ship passes directly over it. By the time the pulse has reflected from the mirror, the rocket ship has moved a short distance toward the mirror. So the astronaut will measure a *shorter* round-trip time and will conclude that the distance was not a yard but something less than a yard. In other words, he says the yardstick has shrunk. And if the rocket ship is moving faster, the astronaut will think that the yardstick has shrunk even more. Note that if the astronaut does the experiment, the man on the ground will think that the yardstick in the rocket has shrunk.

We can make a "clock" by bouncing a light pulse between two mirrors. Our time interval will be the time it takes the pulse to make a round trip (it will be very short unless the mirrors are thousands of miles apart, but this is a "thought experiment"). Just as the first pulse starts out, the rocket ship passes overhead. Because of the relative motion, the astronaut sees a light path for the pulse very different from what a man on the ground sees. In fact the astronaut sees a *longer* light path taking a longer time, so he concludes that the time interval of the clock on the ground is longer than the identical clock in his rocket ship. The clock on the ground, he says, is running slower. Can you see that the man on the ground would say the same thing about the clock in the rocket ship? (See Fig. 4 below.)

The mass of a body increased as its speed increased. When it reached the speed of light, the mass would become infinite—which is impossible. Therefore, no massive body can move at the speed of light—only photons can.

That energy and mass can be changed into one another came from a simple "thought experiment." Einstein wondered what happened to an atom when it lost energy in the form of light. He knew that certain things had to remain the same and from this found that the lost energy could only come from lost mass. His intuition told him that if mass could change into energy, then energy must be able to change into mass. In 1905, this was only a guess. Today, it is seen in all the big accelerators when nuclei collide at high speed.

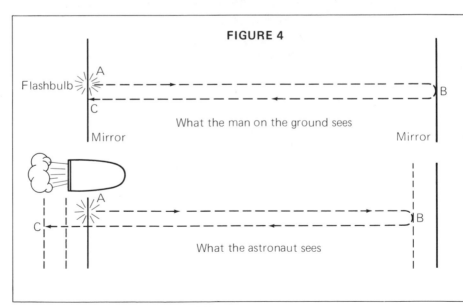

FIGURE 4

Flashbulb
A
B
Mirror
What the man on the ground sees
Mirror

C
A
B
What the astronaut sees

APPENDIX D
THE GENERAL
THEORY OF
RELATIVITY

Einstein wondered what was so special about relative uniform motion. Not every reference system in nature moves in a straight line at a constant speed. What do two observers see when their reference frames—their relative speeds—are changing (acceleration or deceleration)?

Again he did his famous "thought experiments" to guess the answer before he did the mathematics. Suppose a woman is in a windowless room somewhere in space where there is no gravity. She holds out her hand and lets a ball go. Since there is no gravity, the ball hangs in space where she released it. (See Fig. 5.)

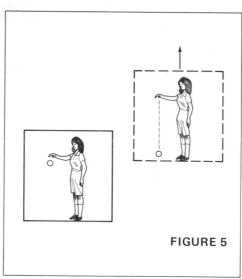

FIGURE 5

Now, unknown to the woman, the room is suddenly accelerated and the floor she is standing on rises. The floor finally meets the ball which is still hanging in space. Since the woman does not know that the room has accelerated up, she thinks the ball has suddenly fallen to the floor. In other words, the ball acted

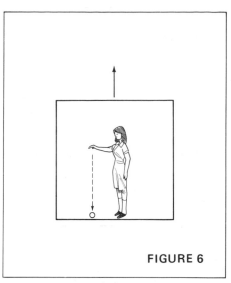

FIGURE 6

as if a gravitational field had suddenly been switched on! But there is still no gravitational field. The only thing that happened was that the room was pulled up. (See Fig. 6 above.)

Einstein concluded that gravity and acceleration had the same effect. You cannot tell the difference between an upward pull and the action of gravity. This is called the "principle of equivalence" since it says the effects due to gravity and acceleration effects are equivalent.

Suppose you have a light beam passing from wall to wall in the closed room. At first, it moves in a straight line and hits the opposite wall. But if the room accelerates upward, the wall will move up while the light is crossing the room. Therefore, the light will hit below its original spot. To the woman, it will seem that the light beam has curved downward. (See Fig. 7, p. 114.)

This means that gravity/acceleration makes a light beam curve. This was to be the most important way of proving the new theory by an experiment.

Now came the mathematics and it turned out to be much more complicated than the simple four dimensions of the special theory. What was involved was not the "flat" Euclidean space, but a curved, non-Euclidean space that required very advanced mathematics.

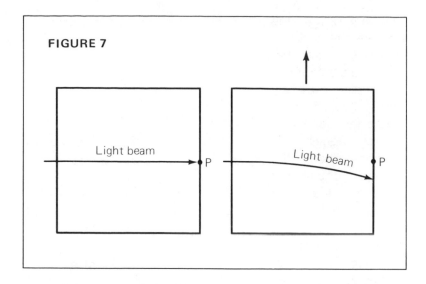

FIGURE 7

Light beam · P

Light beam · P

It is impossible to draw a curved space on a flat sheet of paper, but think of it as something like this:

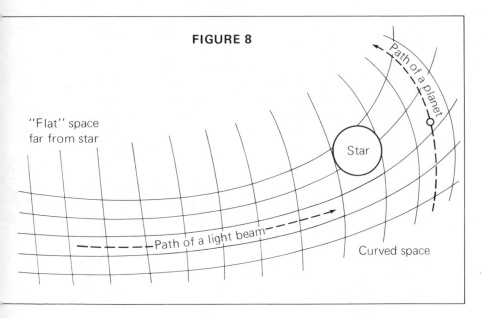

FIGURE 8

Path of a planet

"Flat" space far from star

Star

Path of a light beam

Curved space

Around a massive body, the space is curved. Far from the body, the space is "flat." The path of an object moving in the curved space is one that takes the least time. This is true for light beams as well as planets.

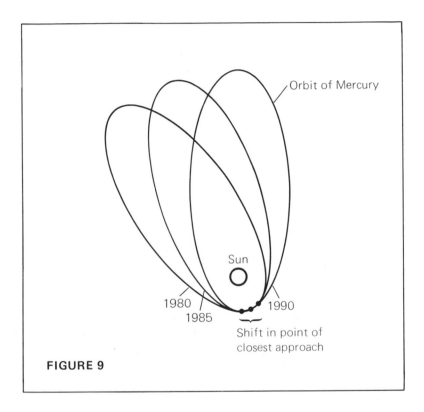

FIGURE 9

The first experimental proof of general relativity was an explanation of the strange behavior of the planet Mercury. It had been known for many years that in going around the sun, Mercury did not return to the same point after one complete revolution. The point of its closest approach to the sun (its perihelion) was slowly moving around Mercury's elliptical orbit. The pull of all the other planets could not account for this. Einstein's relativity gave the correct value for this shift. (See Fig. 9 above.)

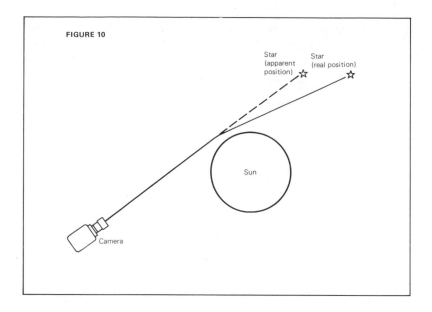

FIGURE 10

The second proof was the deflection of starlight passing near the rim of the sun. This too was a very small change, but it was found by the English eclipse expedition in 1919. (See Fig. 10 above.)

The third proof proposed by Einstein was a shift in the bright lines seen when starlight is analyzed. These he claimed should be moved toward the red part of the spectrum. Although this effect had been seen in 1916, it could not be proved to be the result of relativity. The pressure and temperature changes in stars could have been the cause. It took over fifty years before an experiment on earth confirmed Einstein's prediction.

FOR FURTHER READING

The best popular explanations of Einstein's work were written by Einstein himself. The following books are of interest:

The Evolution of Physics (with L. Infeld). New York: Simon and Schuster, 1938.

The Meaning of Relativity. Princeton, N.J.: Princeton University Press, 1950.

Out of My Later Years. New York: Philosophical Library, 1950.

Relativity. New York: Crown, 1961.

Other books on Einstein's life and work include:

Bernstein, Jeremy. *Einstein*. New York: Viking, 1973.

Clark, Ronald W. *Einstein: The Life and Times*. New York: World Publishers, 1971.

Dukas, Helen and Banesh Hoffmann. *Albert Einstein: The Human Side*. Princeton, N.J.: Princeton University Press, 1979.

Frank, Phillipp. *Einstein, His Life and Times*. New York: Knopf, 1947.

Pais, Abraham. *Subtle is the Lord*. New York: Oxford University Press, 1982.

INDEX